PORT
LLEGE

BASICS

CAD

\\ JAN KREBS \\

BASICS
CAD

BIRKHÄUSER
BASEL·BOSTON·BERLIN

CONTENTS

FOREWORD

Creating design and construction drawings would be inconceivable today without the help of computers. The complexity of major building projects has made it necessary for all participants to be able to exchange data smoothly and to modify layouts regularly in the process of creating the drawing that will ultimately be implemented. Over the past few decades, computer-aided design (CAD) has evolved into a universal tool for planners. CAD programs make it possible to create all documentation, from simple designs to complex construction drawings. They can also display photorealistic depictions or information on quantities and components. Nowadays nearly all architectural and planning offices use the full range of CAD features, and it has become a firm fixture in university studies as well.

Whereas it is possible to buy handbooks and publications that describe the functions of specific CAD programs, what is lacking is a general survey of the basic principles of CAD. Many tips and tricks would be particularly helpful for CAD beginners, keeping them from making basic mistakes that require time-consuming corrections. This is the gap that the Basics student series intends to fill with *Basics CAD*, which provides a fundamental understanding of the functions, processes and structures that all programs share. *Basics CAD* targets first-year students in disciplines such as architecture, engineering, landscape design and interior architecture, as well as trainees in the fields of construction drawing and technical drawing who will work with CAD programs in their later professional environments.

Bert Bielefeld, Editor

CAD: MEANING AND FIELDS OF APPLICATION

CAD – short for computer-aided design – is the catchword for draw-ing and designing with the help of a computer. A wide selection of both simple and complex CAD computer programs (software) makes it possible to create two- and three-dimensional drawings using input devices such as the keyboard, mouse and other tools. These drawings are displayed by output devices such as monitors and printers. The CAD field of IT plays an important role in many areas including engineering. It is used in au-tomotive and plant engineering, as well as in structural engineering and architecture – the focus of this book. Aside from creating technical draw-ings, CAD programs can be used to develop powerful virtual models that provide a basis for a wide range of simulations. CAD programs can gener-ate photorealistic visualizations of buildings, as well as climate and light simulations. With the right CAD software, users can also design load and fluid flow simulations in addition to simplifying development and produc-tion processes.

The first CAD programs were developed in the 1960s and were used primarily in aeroplane construction. With the breakthrough of personal computing and the lower costs of computer workstations in the 1980s, these programs became available to a larger number of users. The power-ful, standardized computing systems developed in the early twenty-first century has led to efficient, relatively inexpensive CAD systems that meet a wide range of requirements.

Although nearly all the programs have a similar foundation, they dif-fer significantly at times in terms of operation and use. There is a great deal of literature on CAD on the market – so much that it is nearly impos-

ᐱ

\\Hint:
In order to establish a practical relationship to application software, *Basics CAD* includes a selection of sample functions from leading CAD software providers in the CAAD (computer-aided architectural design) field. You can find an extensive list of the diverse CAD programs on offer in the appendix of this book.

sible to keep track of – but most of it deals with particular CAD systems. By contrast, the book *Basics CAD* offers a general approach to learning CAD. It contains basic, application-oriented knowledge and is designed to assist the novice in selecting a suitable CAD system.

THE VIRTUAL DRAWING BOARD

When you draw with CAD, the sheet of paper is replaced by the computer monitor, the pencil by the mouse and keyboard. Lines and shapes are created by mouse clicks and keyboard entries, and the whole process is supported by functions that simplify drawing. › Chapter **Drawing elements**

Screen scale

The objects in CAD drawings are usually created on a scale of 1:1 – that is, at their real size. This means that a 10 m wall is drawn with a length of 10 m. To display the entire length of the wall on the screen, you must choose a smaller scale since the space would otherwise not be sufficient to show it. Screen scale describes the ratio between the real size of drawn objects and their depiction on the computer monitor. It changes automatically when the size of the screenshot changes. The actual representational scale that you follow when drawing on paper is created only in the output process in CAD (e.g. printing), but you must always bear it in mind when doing your drawing.

Reference scale

In a CAD drawing on the monitor, this representational scale is referred to as the reference scale. It describes the scale in which the drawn object is likely to be printed (e.g. 1:20, 1:100 or 1:500). Since some of the elements in a drawing, such as lettering, are independent of building components and must be displayed in an appropriate size in subsequent prints, they are not based on a drawing scale of 1:1, but on the probable scale of the printout. This means that, in the drawing operation, the software illustrates on screen the size ratio between the typeface and other elements, including the actual drawn object. › Chapter **Printing and plotting**

\\Tip:
Screen scale must be the same as the reference scale if you wish to view and evaluate the real size of the printout on the screen. Some CAD programs show the screen scale as a percentage of the reference scale: when set at 100% it thus shows the real size of the print. It is also advisable to create sample prints during the work process in order to evaluate the effects of the scale drawing.

\\Hint:
In addition to the mouse and keyboard, you can use a variety of other input devices, including sketchpad and SpaceMouse. However, these play a minor role in architecture-related CAD (see Chapter Hardware).

When technical drawings are made, architects use common units of length so that their work is comprehensible to everyone. In Central Europe, these units are millimetres, centimetres and metres. Some English-speaking countries continue to use feet and inches as units of length, but due to the need for standardization in managing international projects, even these countries are increasingly using the more easily convertible units favoured in Central Europe. You are free to select the units on which you wish to base your CAD drawing. The smallest units can be millimetres, centimetres or metres, or inches or feet.

USER INTERFACE

CAD user interfaces consist of special building blocks that we will explain briefly below by elucidating their underlying concepts.

> 📙

The various tools of the CAD program are displayed by symbols and menus on the user interface. › Fig. 1 You can generate a drawing on the computer using the usual entry devices such as the mouse and the keyboard.

Drawing area

The drawing area is the most important part of the user interface. It allows you to draw and modify objects in either a two-dimensional field or in a space defined in three dimensions. Generally speaking, the CAD drawing area is comparable to a piece of paper. The main difference is that it is a virtual workspace that offers far ranging options and various virtual tools.

Selection and
drawing tools

The computer mouse is a commonly used <u>pointing device</u>. A pointing device controls the cursor on the user interface and functions as a virtual selection and drawing tool. It is represented by an arrow, crosshairs or some other symbol, according to the CAD program in question. This symbol generally changes when you use different selection and drawing options in the drawing operation to indicate the function you are currently using.

Electronic pens

CAD programs allow you to customize electronic pens and specify various line widths, line types and colours. › Fig. 2 You can define line properties before you begin to draw a line, or you can modify them retroactively. This brings greater clarity to both the drawing process and the methodology, since different lines emphasize and illustrate different elements of a drawing. Since many CAD programs link line colours to specific line widths, you can immediately see which elements have been drawn with a specific line width even in complex drawings. In this way, the different elements of a drawing are prepared for subsequent printing based on their

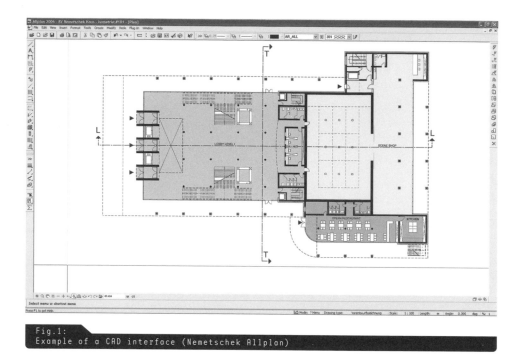

Fig.1:
Example of a CAD interface (Nemetschek Allplan)

screen depiction. > Chapter Printing and plotting The depiction of the pen line represents the subsequent result in the printout.

In addition, many CAD programs allow you to show true-to-scale line widths on the screen. In the corresponding screen scale, the line widths are shown just as they appear in a printout and give an impression of what the print will actually look like. Electronic pens can also be assigned other virtual properties that are important for the visualization of structures. > Chapter Visualization

Menu bar

The menu bar is located above the drawing area and displays the software options in interactive lists. For instance, as is generally the case with Windows-based applications, you can use the "File" menu to create new drawings, open existing ones or store drawing files. Via the menu bar, you can also custom-configure the user interface and activate all software commands and functions by means of the mouse and the keyboard.

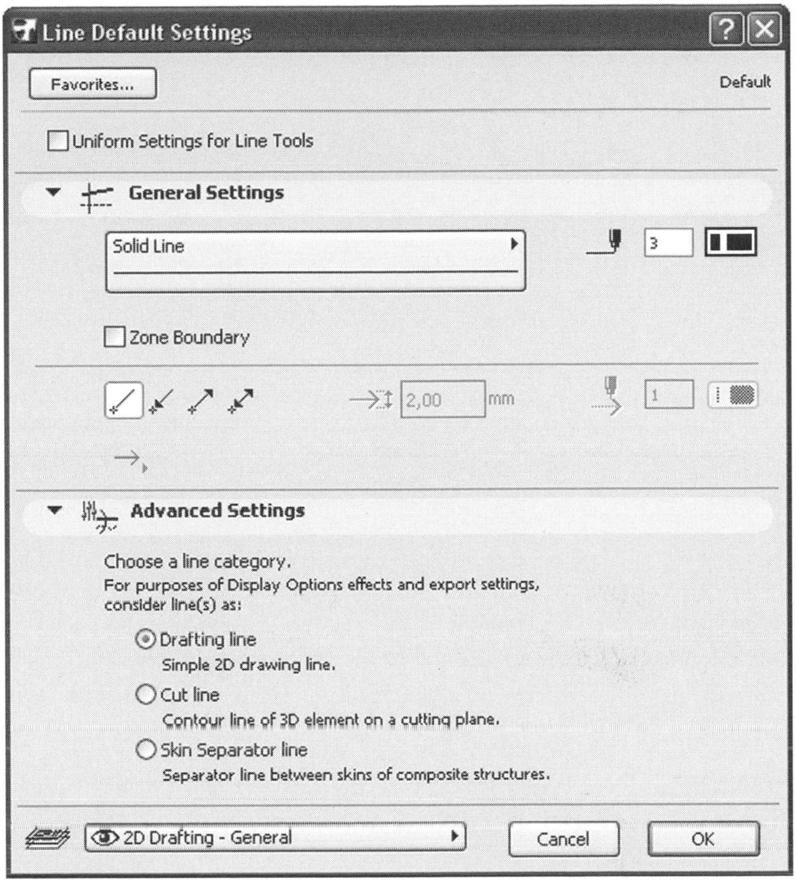

Fig.2:
You can customize the width, type and colour of the lines drawn by electronic pens (Graphisoft ArchiCAD).

Toolbox

The toolbox buttons display symbols of the drawing and tool functions available. They are activated by selection with the virtual selection tool. › Fig. 3 If you move the selection tool to a symbol, the software will usually display the name of the corresponding function. When you use a CAD program for the first time, the user interface will contain default functions that can be configured individually and shown or hidden according to your needs.

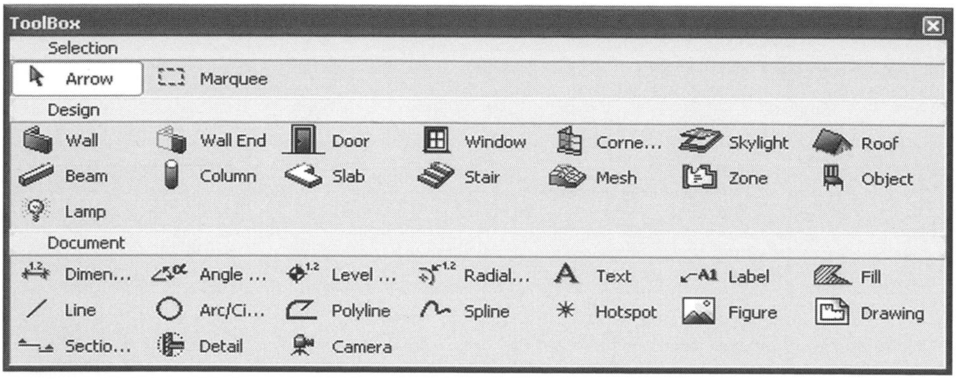

ToolBox

Selection		
Arrow	Marquee	

Design						
Wall	Wall End	Door	Window	Corne...	Skylight	Roof
Beam	Column	Slab	Stair	Mesh	Zone	Object
Lamp						

Document						
Dimen...	Angle ...	Level ...	Radial...	Text	Label	Fill
Line	Arc/Ci...	Polyline	Spline	Hotspot	Figure	Drawing
Sectio...	Detail	Camera				

Fig.3:
Example of a toolbox with various functions (Graphisoft ArchiCAD)

Context menu

Context menus are related to the function you are currently using and contain commands relevant to each drawing operation. In default mode, they can be displayed by right-clicking the mouse, which will make them appear near the drawing and selection tool. Context menus allow you to repeat or cancel commands quickly, and to activate other drawing tools.

Dialogue boxes

A dialogue box allows you to engage in a "dialogue" with the CAD program on a specific function. Dialogue boxes often provide a more detailed description of a selected command, or explain the steps necessary to perform this command. They also make it possible to select special options

\\Tip:
The toolboxes can be displayed in a vertical or horizontal column on the edge of the user interface, or they can be positioned alongside or within the drawing area. An intelligent setup will enlarge the working area and allow you to work more efficiently. Once you have gained some experience of drawing with CAD, you will learn which functions you use frequently, and can then arrange the required toolboxes on the interface so that you can access them quickly.

\\Hint:
Cartesian coordinates are not the only available system. One alternative is the polar coordinate system, in which a point is described by a radius and an angle instead of by X and Y axes.

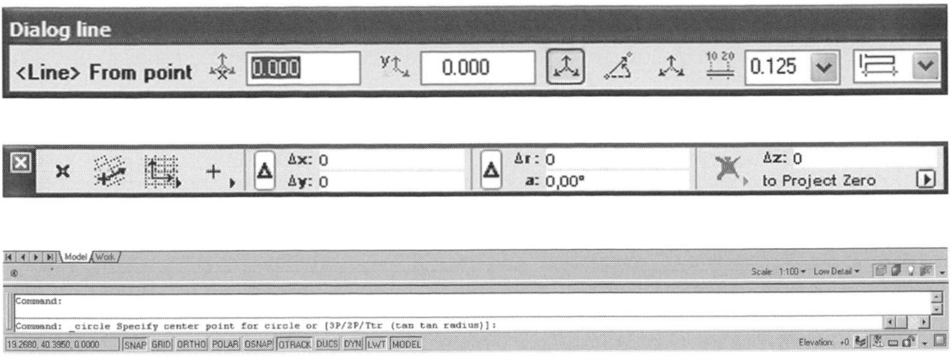

Δx: 0
Δy: 0

Δr: 0
a: 0,00°

Δz: 0
to Project Zero

Model / Work

Scale 1:100 ▾ Low Detail ▾

Command:
Command: circle Specify center point for circle or [3P/2P/Ttr (tan tan radius)]:
19.2680, 40.3950, 0.0000   SNAP GRID ORTHO POLAR OSNAP OTRACK DUCS DYN LWT MODEL   Elevation: +0

Fig.4:
Communicating with CAD software through dialogue boxes (Nemetschek Allplan, Graphisoft ArchiCAD, Autodesk Architectural Desktop)

or to enter numerical values via the keyboard. The boxes are part of the
various drawing and tool functions, and they open automatically on the
user interface when you activate the commands. › Fig. 4

COORDINATE SYSTEMS

The basic geometric reference system in CAD software is a coordi
nate system that defines the virtual drawing area as a construction plane.
This construction plane can be thought of as a piece of graph paper divided
by horizontal and vertical lines. Points on a plane, which are specified as
coordinates, are thus clearly mapped out within the CAD system and can
be used to define the location and shape of drawing elements. › Chapter Drawing elements

The Cartesian coordinate system, which is used most commonly,
is based on two perpendicular axes (X and Y) in two-dimensional space.
These axes describe the distance between any given point and the zero
point of the system. › Fig. 5

Imaginary lines parallel to the X and Y axes intersect within the coordinate system and define the position of any given point.

Going one step further, we can define a line in geometric terms as the
connection between two points. This is also how both endpoints of a line
are specified in the Cartesian coordinate system. › Fig. 6

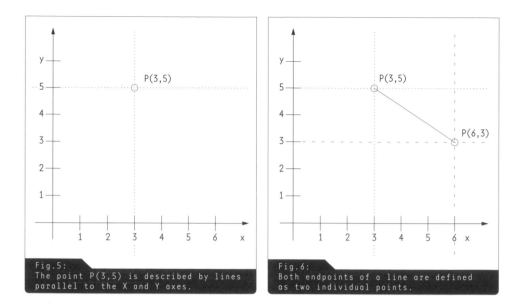

Fig.5:
The point P(3,5) is described by lines parallel to the X and Y axes.

Fig.6:
Both endpoints of a line are defined as two individual points.

Absolute coordinates

Absolute coordinates are based on the above-mentioned zero point of the drawing, at which the X and Y axes intersect. It makes sense to use absolute coordinates when the exact X and Y values of the coordinates you wish to define are known.

User-defined coordinate system

It would be disadvantageous to enter only absolute coordinates together with an absolute, fixed zero point since this would make large drawings particularly difficult to generate using the keyboard.

This is one of the main reasons that most CAD programs allow you to move and thus redefine the point of origin within the coordinate system

\\Hint:
A coordinate system like the one introduced in Figs 5 and 6 is not usually visible on the screen and serves only as an imagined or virtual basis for drawing. In some CAD programs, symbols appear in one corner of the drawing area for orientation purposes and to show the directions of the coordinate axes. They are, however, an exception.

\\ Example:
Apartment walls can be drawn on one layer of a floor plan, the interior furnishings on another. Both levels can be viewed separately, edited or, if necessary, combined (see Fig. 8).

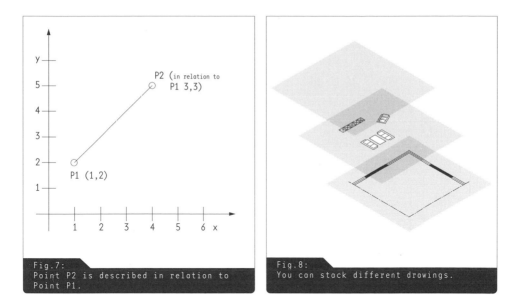

any time you draw new elements. You may also rotate the coordinate system and thus the entire construction plane by any angle of your choosing. This makes it easy to design linear objects that are not perpendicular to the original coordinate system. Below, we refer to such user-defined coordinate systems as UCS.

Relative
coordinates A flexible, alternative method for specifying coordinates incorporates so-called relative coordinates. These are based on the point last defined in the drawing process, which then becomes the temporary reference point for new coordinates. › Fig. 7

TRANSPARENT PLANES – THE LAYERING PRINCIPLE

CAD drawings often contain large amounts of information. As the scope of a drawing expands, so does its complexity, and you might find it increasingly difficult to work on or change elements. This is particularly problematic when many different objects are positioned right next to or on top of one another. CAD programs solve this problem by using variable drawing layers that, like transparent drawing paper, are placed on top of one another as needed. › Fig. 8 These layers may have different names in the various CAD programs. In Nemetschek Allplan, for example, they are called DRAWING FILES.

› ℗

17

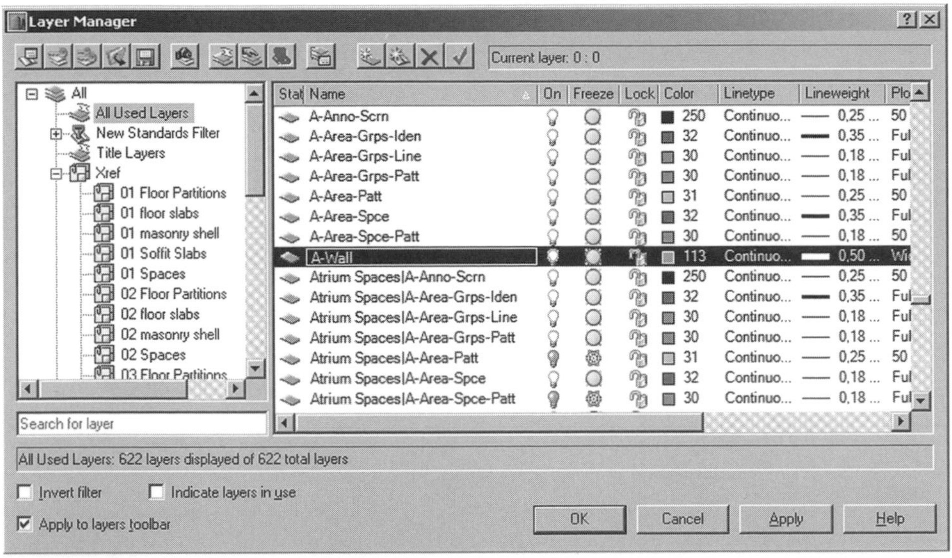

Fig.9:
Example of a CAD layer structure, which enables users to manage different layers and pen properties in a dialogue box (Autodesk Architectural Desktop).

\\Tip:

At the outset of a project, it is worthwhile to give some thought to the way layers – and thus the entire project – need to be organized. For instance, layers can be predefined for different drawing content, even if the layers are used only at a later stage in the project. In addition, if a component consists of several layers, they can be systematically combined to form meaningful overarching layer groups. This approach will allow you to create a hierarchy within a drawing, one that brings the requisite clarity even to complex projects (see Fig. 10).

\\Example:

If two layers are stacked on top of each other, it is possible to see both, but it makes sense to lock one while you continue to work on the other so that you do not inadvertently alter the first one. This is particularly important for complex, multi-layered drawings.

\\Hint:

With many CAD programs (e.g. Graphisoft ArchiCAD), you can structure a drawing not only by layers but also by floors, a feature that is especially useful when designing buildings. The floors are linked to specific elevations and permit a vertical organization of floor plans (based on ground floor, first floor, second floor etc.).

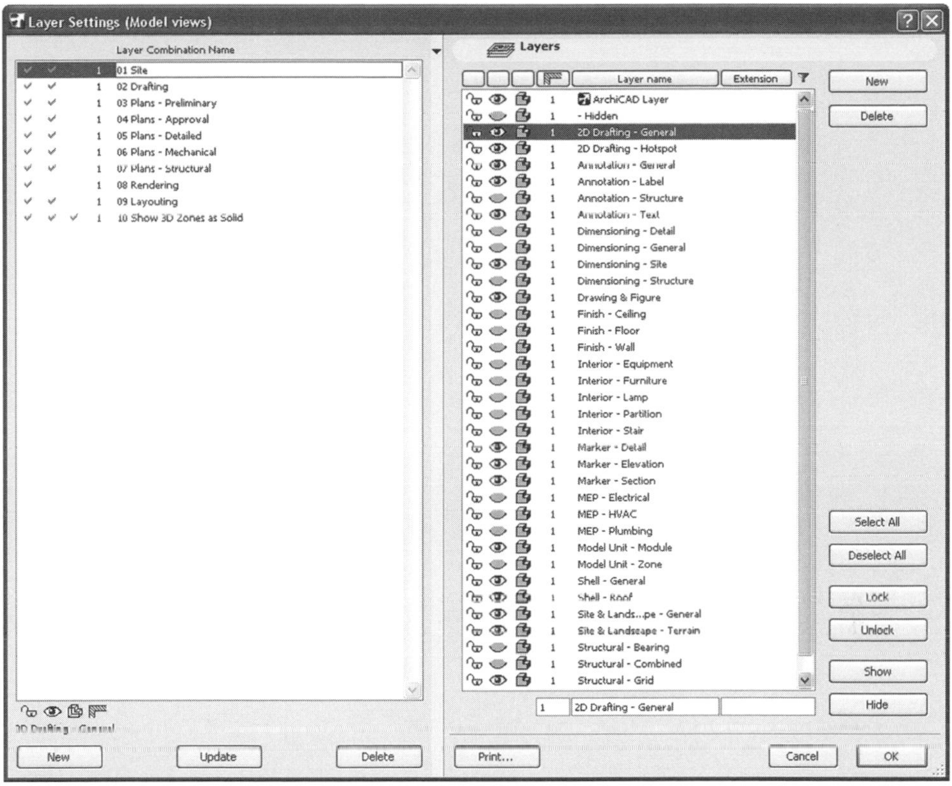

Fig.10:
Creating a hierarchy for drawing content within the layer structure. This brings
clarity to the project (Graphisoft ArchiCAD).

In addition, layer structure plays an important role in organizing a drawing. Using a special dialogue box, you can create any number of layers and manage different drawing content easily. If a structure has many different design elements, this considerably simplifies the design process: independent layers can be created for exterior and interior walls, dimension lines, text, hatching and so on. You can organize drawing contents and retrieve drawings easily. › Fig. 9 and Appendix, Table 1

Further, by creating specific layers, you can show or hide drawing content, or you can "lock" a drawing, making it impossible to alter for a defined period.

The layer system described above not only creates clarity in drawing operations but also allows you to retrieve specific drawing components or general elements quickly and easily when needed. That said, all categorization systems have logical limits or, in certain situations, are not consistently followed. For this reason, many CAD programs also offer a special function that permits users to search for special properties of drawing elements, by either filtering these elements out or activating them. › Fig. 11 This filter function goes by different names in current CAD systems and is sometimes referred to as the FILTER ASSISTANT, or by the more pragmatic term SEARCH AND ACTIVATE. It is normally selected from the menu bar.

\\ Example:
If you have drawn all the exterior walls in a complex floor plan using a special line type, which then proves to be too thick or too thin on a sample print, you can filter out the walls based on their line properties and redefine all of them in just a few short steps. They do not have to be selected individually.

\\ Tip:
The filter function can be used for a great variety of CAD elements. Search criteria include line colour and type, and component specifications (see Chapter Architectural elements). It is useful to draw certain elements or entire components using a specific line colour so that they can easily be filtered out and edited later on.

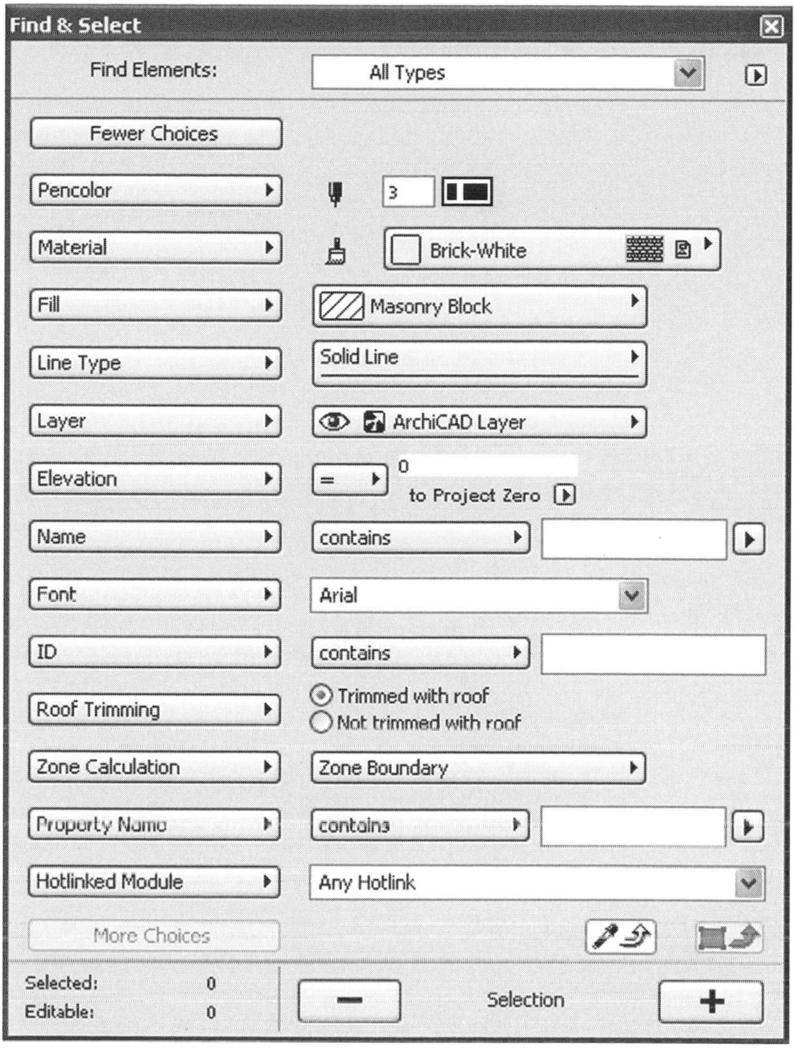

Find & Select ☒

| Find Elements: | All Types ⌄ | ▶ |

Fewer Choices

| Pencolor ▶ | ♟ | 3 | ▐■■ |

| Material ▶ | 🖌 | ☐ Brick-White | ▤ 🖻 ▸ |

| Fill ▶ | ▨ Masonry Block ▶ |

| Line Type ▶ | Solid Line ▶ |

| Layer ▶ | 👁 🔖 ArchiCAD Layer ▶ |

| Elevation ▶ | = ▶ | 0 | to Project Zero ▶ |

| Name ▶ | contains ▶ | | ▶ |

| Font ▶ | Arial ⌄ |

| ID ▶ | contains ▶ | |

| Roof Trimming ▶ | ⊙ Trimmed with roof
○ Not trimmed with roof |

| Zone Calculation ▶ | Zone Boundary ▶ |

| Property Name ▶ | contains ▶ | | ▶ |

| Hotlinked Module ▶ | Any Hotlink ⌄ |

More Choices   🖋⤴   ▮⤴

| Selected: | 0 | | — | Selection | **+** |
| Editable: | 0 |

Fig.11:
Various filter criteria can be used to search for and activate drawing elements (Graphisoft ArchiCAD).

21

DRAWING FUNCTIONS

The design methods introduced in this chapter are basic approaches to drawing sample forms using the related drawing functions. They are popular, simple methods, and we will not treat them exhaustively or touch upon all their variations. Other approaches are possible, depending on the specific features of the program. In CAD there are almost always several ways to reach a destination, and it is important for you to find the quickest, simplest method for your own drawing.

Drawing is supported by CAD commands that make it possible to create the most common geometric elements (points, lines, squares and circles) in an easy, direct process. The various functions can be selected via the symbols displayed in the toolboxes on the user interface. › Fig. 12 and Chapter User interface

Fig.12:
A sample toolbox used to create simple drawing elements such as lines, points, rectangles and circles (Nemetschek Allplan)

\\Tip:
In addition to toolboxes and interactive menus, it is more efficient to use shortcuts to acti-vate drawing and tool functions. Shortcuts are special keyboard combinations linked to specific functions. A well-known shortcut in the Windows operating system is CTRL+C, which copies a file onto the clipboard. The various CAD systems feature a number of default short-cuts that can be quickly adapted to individual needs via the menu bar.

\\Hint:
A polygon is a many-sided object that consists of an enclosed area and a specific number of edges. A polyline is a series of lines and vertices.

DRAWING ELEMENTS

Points

As in a hand drawing, the most basic element in a CAD drawing is a point. In geometric terms, a point is a zero-dimensional object that does not extend into space. All other geometric objects can be described by points and incorporate a particular number of them. For example, two points define a line, three points a triangle, four points a rectangle, eight points a cube and so on. Points are depicted through different symbols in the various CAD programs. › Fig. 13

To draw a point, you must first activate the corresponding drawing function using the POINT command.

With a simple click of the mouse, you can define the position of a point on the construction plane, or you can use the keyboard to enter the X and Y coordinates into the dialogue box. These drawing and entry principles provide a foundation for all the drawing functions described below, and they make it possible to create any desired shape – though at times a number of intermediate steps may be involved.

Lines

A simple straight line is described by two points. After you fix a point on the construction plane using the LINE command, you need to specify a second point as the endpoint. The CAD program then creates the line in the desired position. › Fig. 14

Polylines

A polyline consists of several line segments connected to create a coherent object. › Fig. 15

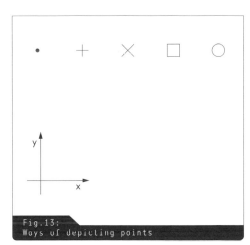

Fig.13:
Ways of depicting points

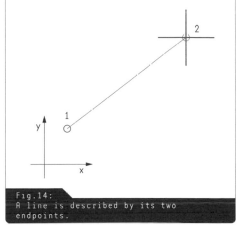

Fig.14:
A line is described by its two endpoints.

23

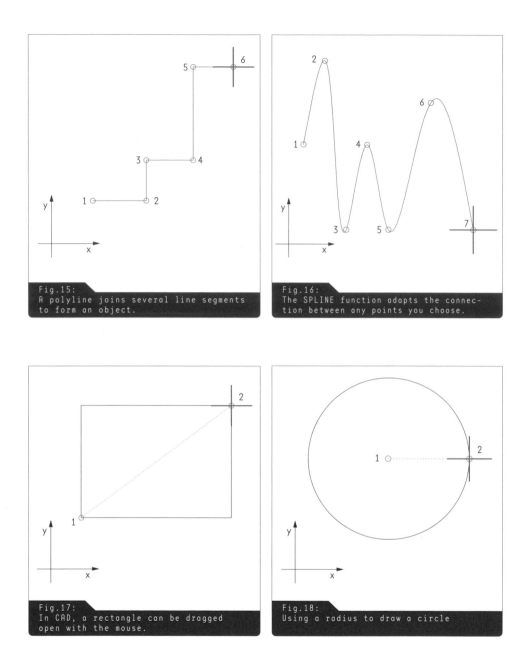

Fig.15:
A polyline joins several line segments to form an object.

Fig.16:
The SPLINE function adapts the connection between any points you choose.

Fig.17:
In CAD, a rectangle can be dragged open with the mouse.

Fig.18:
Using a radius to draw a circle

Splines   The term "spline" comes from shipbuilding, where it is used to describe a pliant board that is anchored at several points and bent to fit the curvature of a ship's hull. The corresponding drawing function works in

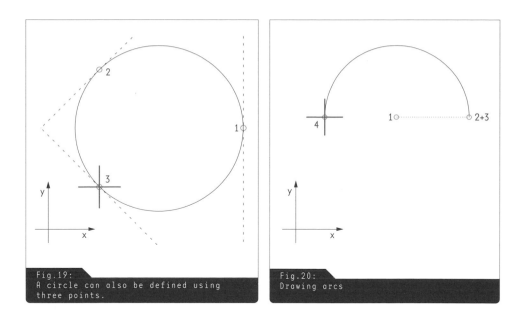

Fig.19:
A circle can also be defined using
three points.

Fig.20:
Drawing arcs

the same way. It interpolates curves between arbitrary points, creating
soft, flowing shapes. › Fig. 16

Squares and
rectangles

A rectangle does not need to be drawn in a complicated fashion using four individual lines. It can be created much more easily via a single
function. One method is to draw the rectangle using its diagonal. › Fig. 17
You can either drag it open with the mouse or enter its parameters with
the keyboard.

Circles

There are various ways to define a circle. To begin with, you can describe it by its radius. In this case, you enter its centre into the dialogue
box of the CIRCLE command. Then you specify the desired radius with the
mouse-controlled drawing tool or enter a numerical value into the dialogue
line using the keyboard. › Fig. 18 In other CAD programs, you can draw a
circle by defining its diameter or three points on its perimeter, by using
tangents, or by combining these methods of specifying points on a plane.
› Fig. 19

Circular arcs

The arc is another important drawing element. Using the CIRCLE command, you can create either an entire circle or a section of it. If you wish
to draw an arc, first define the centre and radius, then specify the arc's
beginning and endpoint. › Fig. 20

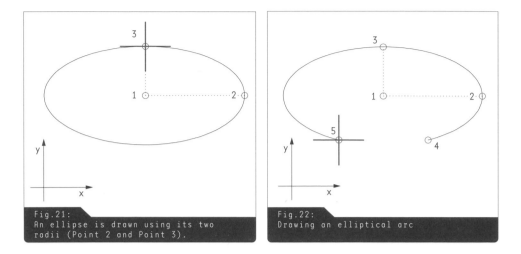

Fig.21:
An ellipse is drawn using its two
radii (Point 2 and Point 3).

Fig.22:
Drawing an elliptical arc

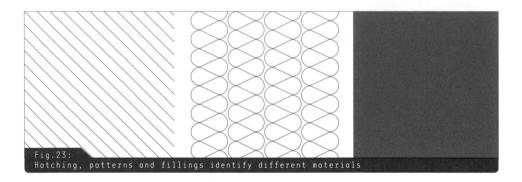

Fig.23:
Hatching, patterns and fillings identify different materials

Ellipses

Ellipses are drawn in the same way as circles. The only difference is that both radii must be specified after the centre is defined. › Fig. 21

Elliptical arcs

An elliptical arc is created in the same way as an ellipse, but requires a beginning and an endpoint as well. › Fig. 22

Hatching, patterns and fillings

Using hatching, patterns and fillings makes it easy to represent surfaces and enhances the legibility of individual drawing elements. › Fig. 23 Hatching provides information on the properties of both the materials and building components used in the design. Patterns and fillings allow an abstract depiction of surfaces and can also be used for the graphical pres-

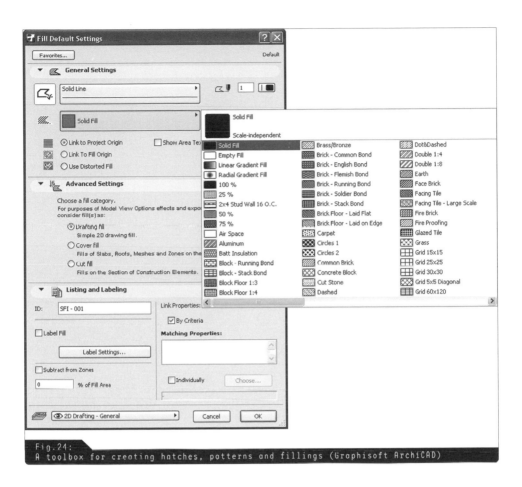

Fig.24:
A toolbox for creating hatches, patterns and fillings (Graphisoft ArchiCAD)

entation of drawings. Not all CAD programs distinguish between hatching, patterns and fillings. Many display all these functions in a single toolbox.
> Fig. 24

After selecting the desired surface by clicking the matching symbol, it can be "drawn" in a number of ways. You can enter each corner point of the depicted surface one after the other, or generate a rectangular surface using its diagonal, as in the process of creating a square. > page 25

Automatic
boundary
detection

Many CAD programs offer an alternative method for enclosed fig-ures: if the outer perimeter of an object completely surrounds its inner

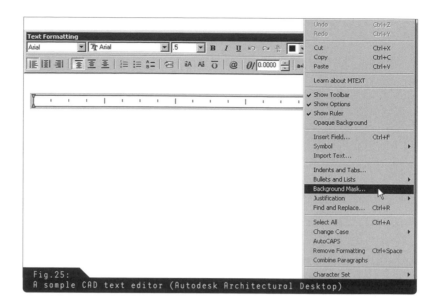

Fig.25:
A sample CAD text editor (Autodesk Architectural Desktop)

> area, you can activate the <u>automatic boundary detection</u> function, which is usually located on the menu bar.

After this function is activated, the software inspects the surrounding contour line and fills in the selected surface. This saves a great deal of time, particularly when objects have complex geometries or a large number of corners.

Text elements   In many CAD programs, you can add text to drawings using a text editor. Like the common word-processing programs, this editor can be

\\Tip:
Automatic boundary detection works only for completely enclosed areas. If a drawing is imprecise, the contour lines may have small gaps that might not be visible when displayed on the screen in a normal size. Subsequent attempts to find the error can be time-consuming. For this reason – and for other drawing functions that build on one another – it is important to create precise drawings if you want to efficiently exploit the benefits of CAD.

\\Hint:
A precisely defined reference elevation, on which all higher or lower elevation points are based, is essential to ensure the correct relationship between the elevation points. This reference elevation is normally represented by the finished floor level (FFL) of the building's ground floor, and it equals ±0.00 m.
Additional information on dimension lines in particular and technical drawing in general can be found in *Basics Technical Drawing* by Bert Bielefeld and Isabella Skiba, Birkhäuser Publishers, Basel, 2006.

28

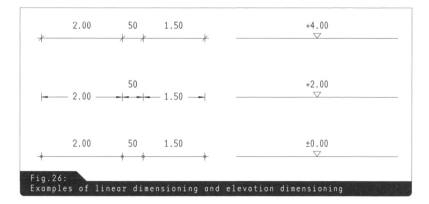

Fig.26:
Examples of linear dimensioning and elevation dimensioning

used to change various parameters, including font type and character size. › Fig. 25 After activating the editor, you enter text word by word or copy it from other programs (e.g. Microsoft Word) using the standard copy function. However, some CAD programs do not have a text editor with a special entry window. In this case, you enter text directly into the drawing area and select it there for subsequent editing.

Dimension lines

Even though technical drawings are usually drawn to a particular scale, you should define all the relevant dimensions of a drawing. This can be done with dimension chains, elevation points and individual dimensions.

Linear
dimensioning

The linear dimensioning function allows you to add dimension lines to horizontal, vertical and diagonal elements. First, you select, in any order, the points that need to be dimensioned. After you execute the function, the CAD program automatically generates the dimension lines and positions them in the desired location with the matching arrowheads, numbers and, if necessary, text. › Fig. 26, left These parameters can be set and subsequently edited in a dialogue box. Dimension points can also be entered into or deleted from existing dimension chains. The software independently computes all new distances.

Elevation
dimensioning

Elevations in views and sections are also defined by elevation points. These are represented by an equilateral triangle and displayed directly in the drawing along with numerals. This dimensioning method is intended to measure and display height differences only. › Fig. 26, right The important points are simply clicked with the mouse, and a reference elevation is selected. Afterward the CAD program calculates the elevation and displays it at the chosen spot.

› ◖

DESIGN TOOLS

The design tools introduced in this chapter are stand-ins for the large number of available options in CAD programs, where they depend on the individual software configurations. They are not necessarily identical in these different CAD programs, nor do they work in the same way. You will need to learn the special functions of the CAD program you choose and familiarize yourself with its special features. Ultimately, choosing a suitable CAD system depends not only on product quality but also on your own particular way of drawing.

Grids

Grids play an important role in the design of structures. They bring clarity to the work, particularly when large objects are involved, and provide critical support for the design process. For instance, a support grid can simplify the process of designing a building's loadbearing structure, and an axis grid can make it easier to design façades. Grids can be used for these same purposes in CAD and are a constructive drawing tool as well. › Fig. 27

Snap functions

To create accurate drawings, you must draw objects using precisely defined points. Using coordinates › Chapter Coordinate systems you can enter these points via the keyboard. Even so, the mouse is a much quicker and more intuitive entry tool for CAD drawings. The snap function, accessed via the menu bar or special toolboxes, allows you to select a point precisely with the virtual drawing and marking tool and prevents you from erring by a few millimetres within the drawing. It "snaps" onto drawing elements – that is, it selects them with great precision. The above-mentioned grid points can also serve as snap points: if you move the drawing tool close to one of these points on the screen, the CAD software marks it with a symbol. If you then execute the LINE command, specifying the starting point of a line with a mouse click, it will become the snap point. › Fig. 28 This ensures the necessary precision for drawing.

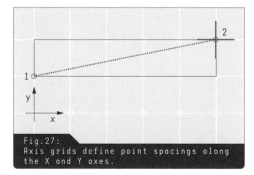

Fig. 27:
Axis grids define point spacings along the X and Y axes.

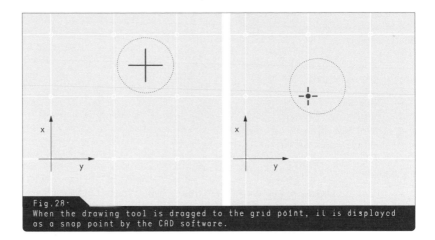

The snap function usually works only in conjunction with other drawing commands. The required command must first be selected if you want the CAD software to activate the snap points automatically once they are within the drawing tool's snap radius.

Object snap

Snap points may be used in various ways. They may incorporate the end and mid points of lines, the corners of squares, the centres of circles, the intersection points of two objects and so on. › Figs 29–31 A symbol, displayed temporarily, illustrates the proximity of a potential snap point to the drawing tool – similar to the process of snapping onto grid points. The snap radius defines the maximum distance within which the drawing tool activates the snap point. Hence, the required snap point is temporarily activated once it is enclosed by an imaginary circle around a specific point whose radius usually measures a few millimetres on the screen.

\\Tip:
A grid consists of points, at user-defined distances, which can be connected with lines. For instance, a grid can be formed by the same sized spaces corresponding to 1 m on the X and Y axes. In CAD, grids can be arbitrarily moved within a drawing, just like the zero point of the underlying user-defined coordinate system (UCS).

\\Hint:
Precision is crucial when drawing with CAD, since coordinates and drawing elements are usually linked, and even small mistakes made at the beginning of a drawing can quickly become magnified as the work continues.

31

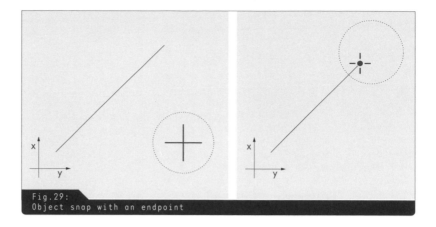

Fig.29:
Object snap with an endpoint

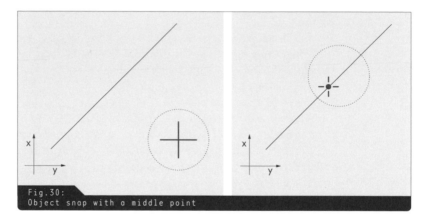

Fig.30:
Object snap with a middle point

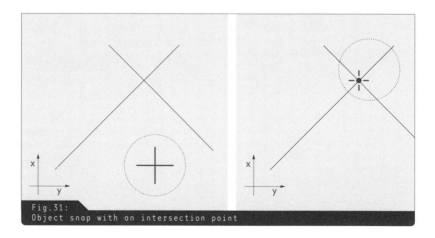

Fig.31:
Object snap with an intersection point

Precise angle specifications are one of the most important criteria for creating precise technical drawings. CAD programs create precise angles in different ways. They usually allow you to specify the desired angle in a dialogue box via the keyboard or an interactive angle-degree selector. In many CAD programs, you are also given the option of an angle snap command with predefined angle increments if you hold down the shift key while drawing. Additional tool functions can normally be used as drawing aids and are available in toolboxes. › **Figs 32–35**

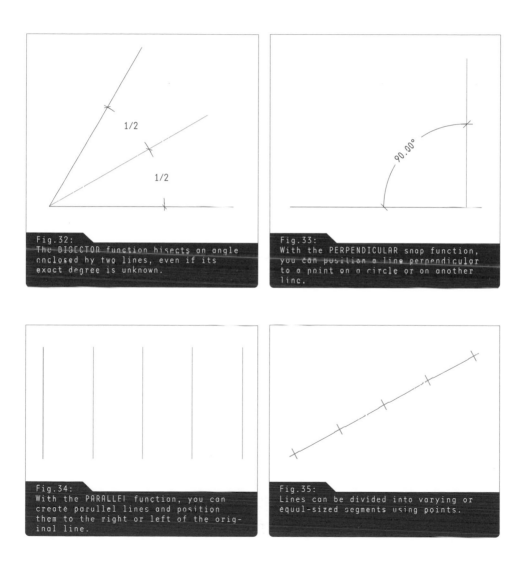

Fig. 32:
The BISECTOR function bisects an angle enclosed by two lines, even if its exact degree is unknown.

Fig. 33:
With the PERPENDICULAR snap function, you can position a line perpendicular to a point on a circle or on another line.

Fig. 34:
With the PARALLEL function, you can create parallel lines and position them to the right or left of the original line.

Fig. 35:
Lines can be divided into varying or equal-sized segments using points.

MODIFICATIONS

One of the great advantages of CAD is that it allows you to edit and change objects after they have been drawn. This means that, in the design process, you can execute modifications and optimizations with relatively little effort. You can also, if necessary, modify templates and adjust them to meet a variety of requirements. There is no need to recreate every drawing from scratch, and it is possible to streamline the generation of standard objects. > Chapter Program libraries

Associativity

CAD elements can be "associatively" modified. For instance, if you fill a square with hatching and subsequently change its shape, the hatching automatically follows its new perimeter. > Fig. 36 The square and its filling are linked and geometrically dependent on each other. Another example of associativity is a component that is altered in combination with dimensioning lines: if the length of the component is modified, the corresponding dimension chains automatically change too – provided there is an associative link between the two. This means that it is not necessary to create new dimension lines for an edited component that has already been dimensioned.

Grouping

In CAD, objects are often made up of various elements that form a unit in the drawing but are not necessarily linked. For instance, the drawing of a bed may consist of several lines, which must be individually selected if they are modified. Here, it is possible to group together several elements so that you do not need to activate all of them when you select an object. Depending on the CAD system used, they are combined to create GROUPS, BLOCKS or SEGMENTS. Defined as such, they form units that can be broken up again if necessary. This normally makes the work much easier.

Modifying points

The process of drawing objects becomes much more flexible because users are able to modify individual points or several points at the same time. Simple changes in line length can be made with the mouse, and sur-

---

\\Tip:
An existing building layout can easily be modified by selecting all the points on one side of the building and moving them in the desired direction within the UCS. All the selected points will move as well, and the lines and components will automatically be lengthened.

\\Hint:
When you make other types of modifications, it is also helpful to use a selection window to activate elements because this tool provides greater control in selecting and changing elements.

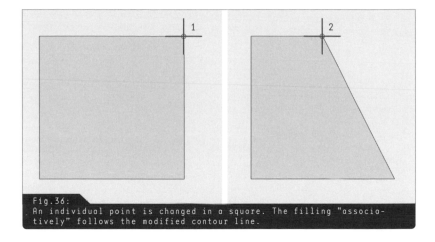

Fig.36:
An individual point is changed in a square. The filling "associatively" follows the modified contour line.

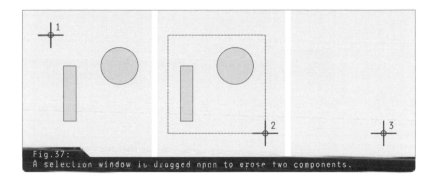

Fig.37:
A selection window is dragged open to erase two components.

faces and three-dimensional objects can also be altered easily. › Chapter The
third dimension

After activating the command, you can, for instance, grasp the corner
of a rectangle using the snap function and move it to the desired position
within the virtual drawing area. › Fig. 36

Erase

The erase function is executed using the selection tool. It can be used
to remove any element in the drawing completely, or to erase several elements at once. After activating the erase function, you simply drag open a
window with the mouse. Depending on the basic settings, you can erase all
objects that are located within the selection window or that are intersected
by it. › Fig. 37

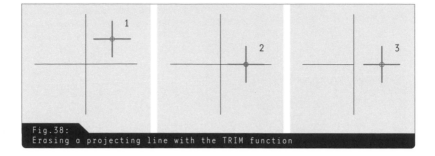

Fig.38:
Erasing a projecting line with the TRIM function

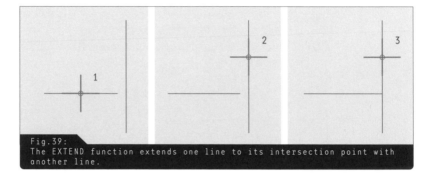

Fig.39:
The EXTEND function extends one line to its intersection point with another line.

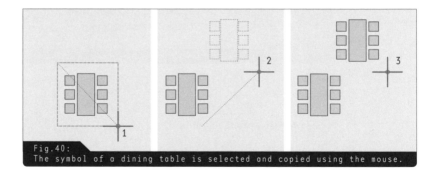

Fig.40:
The symbol of a dining table is selected and copied using the mouse.

\\Tipp:
You can usually use the TRIM and EXTEND functions for either a single line or for several lines. Hence, any number of lines can be selected, trimmed and extended at the same time.

\\Tip:
Snap points can also be used to grasp an object. They allow you to snap onto the object and move it to another location with great accuracy. Snap points can also be used to position it there.

Trimm

It is also possible to trim or remove parts of elements. With the trim function (also called SHORTEN or DELETE ELEMENT BETWEEN POINTS in some CAD systems), a line segment running between two points or extending beyond a single point can be erased by activating the function and clicking the line segment with the selection and drawing tool. › Fig. 38

Extend
›

The opposite command, EXTEND (also called LENGTHEN or CONNECT TWO ELEMENTS), extends a line to its intersection point with another line. › Fig. 39

Copy

The COPY function is one of the most important drawing commands and forms the basis of an efficient work process. Generally speaking, before redrawing an object, you should always consider whether a drawn object can first be copied and then changed. This is especially true of complex objects that are time-consuming to create, whether these are objects you draw yourself or library elements. › Chapter Program libraries

To copy an object, first select it and then drag it to the desired location by holding down the selection and drawing tool. The original object will remain in its initial position. › Fig. 40

Mirror

You can use the MIRROR function to create mirror-images of objects along any axis you choose. You can also create a copy – which is naturally inverted – and continue to use the original. After activating the command and selecting the object, you specify a mirror axis at the desired distance and angle to the original and then mirror the object across the chosen axis. You can also use lines and edges of existing elements as mirror axes.

In combination with the copy function, this command makes it possible to draw symmetrical objects efficiently: only one half must be drawn, and the other half can be mirrored across the middle axis. › Fig. 41

\\ Example:
If you are drawing the floor plan of a twin house, you can mirror either all or a part of the layout across the middle axis before continuing with your work. The same approach lends itself well to drawing façades and other building components quickly and efficiently.

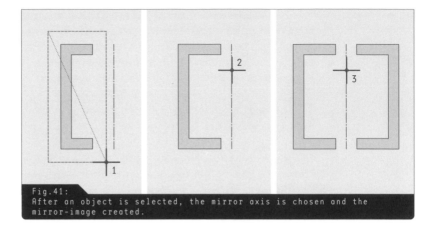

Fig.41:
After an object is selected, the mirror axis is chosen and the mirror-image created.

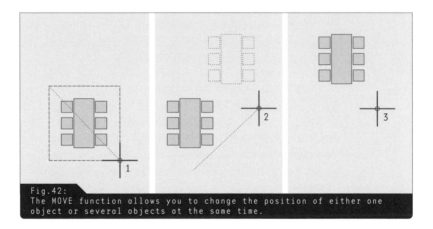

Fig.42:
The MOVE function allows you to change the position of either one object or several objects at the same time.

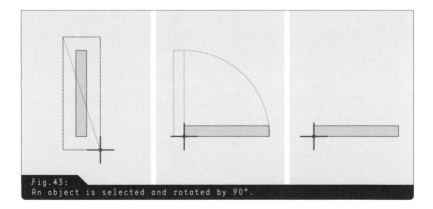

Fig.43:
An object is selected and rotated by 90°.

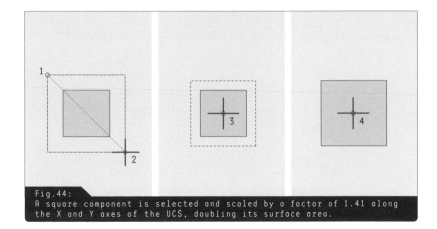

Fig.44:
A square component is selected and scaled by a factor of 1.41 along
the X and Y axes of the UCS, doubling its surface area.

Move

The MOVE function is quite similar to the copy function. The only difference is that the object is moved and no copy is made. › Fig. 42

Rotate

With the ROTATE function, drawn objects can be rotated an arbitrary distance around an arbitrarily selected point. If all that is needed is to change the object's orientation, its middle point represents an ideal snap point. With the mouse, you specify the original angle – normally the positive X axis in the UCS. Starting here, the object is then rotated around its centre. Alternatively, you can use the keyboard to enter the rotation angle after determining its pivot point. This method can be employed to rotate a vertical structure by 90°. › Fig. 43

Scale and
stretch

The size, length and shape of all drawn objects can be changed with great accuracy. The SCALE or STRETCH function allows you to scale an object in all directions of the coordinate system. › Fig. 44

THE THIRD DIMENSION

The preceding chapters dealt primarily with drawing functions on the construction plane, which, from a geometric perspective, is the equivalent of a two-dimensional sheet of drawing paper. One great advantage of CAD systems is that they allow you to work in space, that is, in three dimensions.

Whereas a drawing only reproduces a view of a 2D structure, three-dimensional design in CAD allows the designer to give shape to the 3D object. A Z axis must be added to the basic CAD reference system – the coordinate system – in order to transform a two-dimensional plane into three-dimensional space. The most commonly used coordinate system is the Cartesian system discussed above, which is merely expanded to include the Z axis. The Z axis rises perpendicularly from the zero point of the plane defined by the X and Y axes and makes it possible to define the point P(3,5) from Fig. 5, page 16, in three-dimensional space. › **Fig. 45**

THREE-DIMENSIONAL DESIGN
In the third dimension, the two-dimensional construction plane becomes an element of the three-dimensional workspace. However, as a rule,

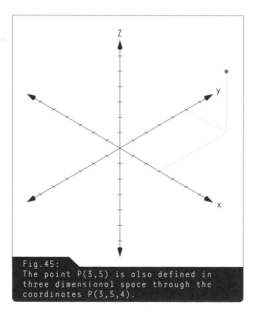

Fig.45:
The point P(3,5) is also defined in
three dimensional space through the
coordinates P(3,5,4).

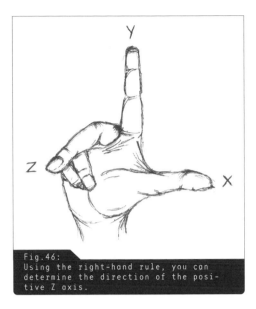

Fig.46:
Using the right-hand rule, you can determine the direction of the positive Z axis.

use of this workspace normally relies on two-dimensional pointing and output devices such as a mouse and a screen. This can take some getting used to when complicated, three-dimensional drawings are involved.

Projections Whereas two-dimensional drawings generally only involve the projection of a plane (e.g. floor plan or view), three-dimensional representations allow you to alternate between the top or bottom view, the four different elevations and the isometric representations. › Fig. 47 All these presentation methods create projections of the same three-dimensional objects and

\\Tip:
The "right-hand-rule" can help you get your bearings within the Cartesian coordinate system. If the directions of the X and Y axes in a three-dimensional coordinate system are known, this rule shows the direction of the positive Z axis. If the thumb and index finger of your right hand point in the positive X and Y directions, your extended middle finger represents the positive Z axis (see Fig. 46).

\\Tip:
When designing, you should start thinking and working in three dimensions as early as possible, since many of the links and relationships within a structure are best checked in spatial terms. Along with simple cardboard models, abstract virtual 3D mass models are particularly useful, since they can be constructed relatively easily and provide quick results (see Chapters Construction methods and Visualization).

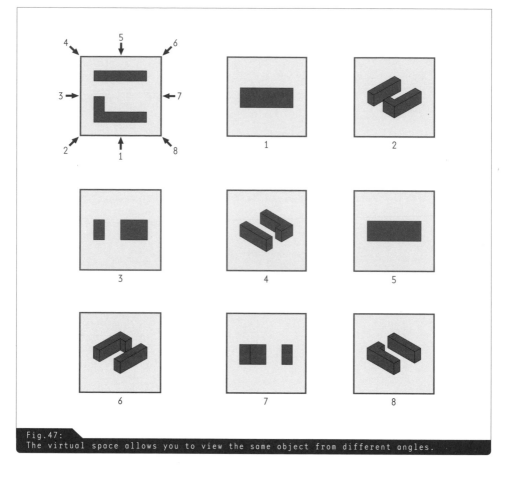

Fig. 47:
The virtual space allows you to view the same object from different angles.

facilitate both clear spatial presentation in the respective viewing mode and the editing of particular points of a 3D design. Most CAD programs allow you to view several projections simultaneously in different windows on the screen. You are thus able to see the object from all directions.

Models

Three-dimensionally defined objects have different qualities and, depending on the design method used, can be categorized as volume models, plane models or edge models.

Volume models

A volume body is a solid object that contains a great deal of information within the CAD system. › Fig. 48 As well as providing volumes and the information derived from them such as mass and centre of gravity, volume

42

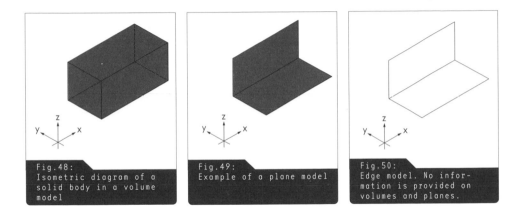

Fig.48:
Isometric diagram of a solid body in a volume model

Fig.49:
Example of a plane model

Fig.50:
Edge model. No information is provided on volumes and planes.

models can be used to define surface characteristics and specific materials. › Chapter Visualization This enables the production of a virtual image of a structural component that exhibits the same characteristics under programmable virtual conditions as its real counterpart. Moreover, the image allows for interpolations, which can be geometrically defined within the volume. This makes it possible for bodies to be geometrically combined, subtracted from one another or positioned to form intersections. › Chapter Modelling

Plane models

› 🗋

As their name suggests, plane models consist exclusively of planes and do not have any defined volume. In the CAD program planes can be defined in terms of the visual characteristics of their surfaces, and they can be rotated and inclined at any angle within the virtual workspace. › Fig. 49

Edge model

An edge model uses three dimensional lines to simulate only the edges of a body. No information is provided concerning surfaces or volumes,

> 🗋
> \\Hint:
> Plane models can enclose a volume without the latter being geometrically defined like a volume model. This produces objects whose shell provides information on surface characteristics and may resemble a volume model. Nevertheless, this shell consists exclusively of two-dimensional planes without material thickness. The object is just a hollow body.

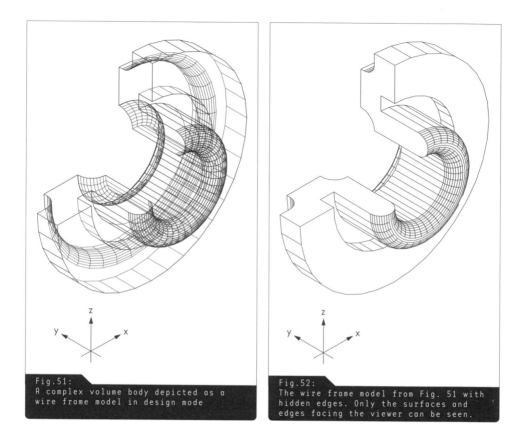

Fig.51:
A complex volume body depicted as a
wire frame model in design mode

Fig.52:
The wire frame model from Fig. 51 with
hidden edges. Only the surfaces and
edges facing the viewer can be seen.

which are thus not geometrically defined. Edge models play only a minor role in architectural CAD since they are highly abstract representations. › Fig. 50

Wire frame model   In the 3D design mode of most CAD programs it is standard for all spatial objects to be depicted as wire frame models in order to take all point coordinates into account.

A wire frame model – which should not be confused with the edge model described above – is a skeletal depiction of a 3D object using three-dimensionally defined lines. In the design mode, both volume and plane models are shown as wire frame models, although in this special type of constructive representation information about volumes and planes is not included. In the virtual workspace a wire frame representation can be observed from any chosen point, allowing you to check spatial relationships such as the distances between structural components and overlaps. Some practice is required to be able to differentiate between "front" and "back" in a complex wire frame model, because the model shows spatial depth even though a two-dimensional representation appears on the monitor. › Fig. 51 Some CAD programs function without the depiction of wire frame models and visualize three-dimensional objects directly with shaded or coloured surfaces.

Hidden edges
If required, all edges located behind three-dimensional objects and planes can be concealed to provide better orientation within the drawing. This makes the representation much more comprehensible and is a preliminary stage in computer rendering, although in contrast to a completed visualization it can still be modified. › Fig. 52 and Chapter Visualization Other CAD programs give the command for this representation option as HIDE or HIDDEN LINE.

Generating floor plans, views and sections
Technical drawings typically depict floor plans, views and sections of entire structures or structural components as detail drawings. However, in three-dimensional design mode you can produce complete virtual models that, if necessary, can provide a basis for generating the two-dimensional figures of a technical drawing.

Floor plans and horizontal sections
In default mode, the construction plane of a CAD system is represented as a top view, i.e. the user looks down on the XY plane of the UCS and thus onto a virtual model. In order to represent a particular floor of a virtual building as a floor plan, a horizontal section plane is generated

\\Tip:
Calculating the dimensions of hidden lines can be time-consuming. Where the scale and detail of a 3D representation has been clearly specified prior to the construction of the 3D model, you should, where applicable, avoid irrelevant elements and unnecessary depth of detail. If you require a 3D model for both a rough representation and a detailed depiction, details such as doorknobs should be represented on an additional layer so that they can be excluded from the calculations relevant to the rough model (see Chapters Transparent planes – the layering principle and Visualization).

\\Hint:
Along with a design mode window, many CAD programs also offer an optional 3D depiction. This can be activated as an additional window and can show three-dimensional objects with hidden edges and shaded or coloured surfaces. Objects depicted in this way can usually be rotated and examined from all sides.

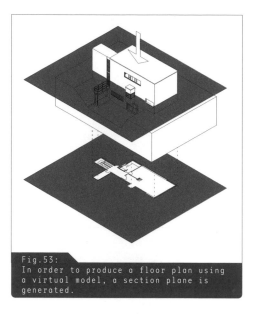

Fig.53:
In order to produce a floor plan using
a virtual model, a section plane is
generated.

> 📎
> ✎

which slices through all walls and objects within the building at a particular height and thus depicts them as elements of a floor plan. › **Fig. 53**

Views and vertical sections

Most CAD programs employ the same tool functions to generate views and sections. In technical drawing, a section is also a view: one that cuts through a building or component, thus allowing you to see the interior of the object. In contrast to the generation of a floor plan, longitudinal and lateral cuts produce vertical sections, which slice through an object in a

📎

\\Hint:
The drawings in Figs 53–55 are based on a design by Le Corbusier for an apartment block in Vaucresson (1922), although the dimensions and details do not correspond exactly to the original.

✎

\\Tip:
A horizontal section cuts through objects parallel to the XY plane of the UCS. It follows that a vertical section bisects objects parallel to the Z axis. Some CAD programs provide predefined horizontal section planes as floor levels (e.g. Graphisoft ArchiCAD), and you can alternate between these while working on the different floor plans of a building (see Chapter Transparent planes – the layering principle).

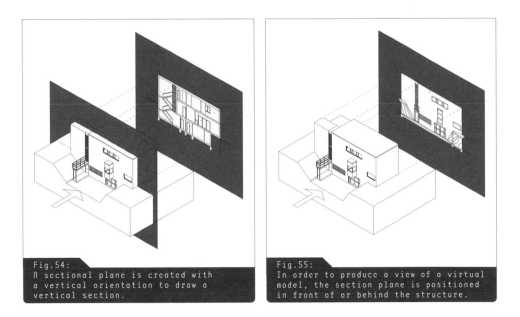

Fig.54:
A sectional plane is created with a vertical orientation to draw a vertical section.

Fig.55:
In order to produce a view of a virtual model, the section plane is positioned in front of or behind the structure.

longitudinal or lateral direction. The first step is to establish the length as well as the line and depth of vision of the section plane. (In the case of a view, this section plane is located in front of or behind an object.) Within the top view, the CAD software then generates the symbol for a section boundary, which you can select to access a depiction of the defined section or view. Depending on the CAD system used, this depiction is shown in a special section-view window or is generated as a two-dimensional drawing, which you can then work on. › Figs 54 and 55

\\Hint:
Some programs allow you to create and label a view or section and assign it a separate window even though the relevant virtual model is still linked with 3D data (e.g. Graphisoft ArchiCAD). As a result, when you work on elements in construction mode, any changes you make are automatically reflected associatively in the projection. Alternatively, the projection can be generated on an additional layer consisting only of two-dimensional lines.

CONSTRUCTION METHODS

Three-dimensional construction methods function similarly to two-dimensional drawing commands. That said, there is a fundamental difference: coordinates are not only defined via the X and Y axes but are also positioned in space using the Z axis. › Chapter Three-dimensional design

Points, lines and planes in space

As when drawing points, lines and planes in the construction plane of the UCS, you use a drawing function to draw them in three-dimensional space. Working within a spatial projection takes some getting used to, since you are often unable to see the real lengths of spatial representations, because not all objects are shown parallel to the coordinate axes and thus appear shortened or elongated in different projections. › Fig. 56

›✎

Cuboids

Simple bodies can be generated as volume models with the drawing functions. For example, a cuboid is initially defined by its base or base area by using its diagonal and then assigned a height. › Fig. 57 The base is always positioned on the construction plane and is parallel to the XY plane of the UCS.

Cylinders

A cylinder can have either a circular or an elliptical base. Once this has been defined, the height of the cylinder is determined using the Z axis. › Fig. 58

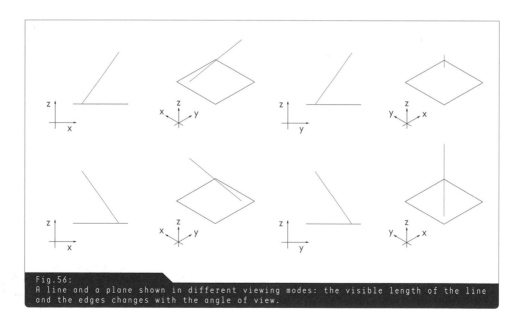

Fig. 56:
A line and a plane shown in different viewing modes: the visible length of the line and the edges changes with the angle of view.

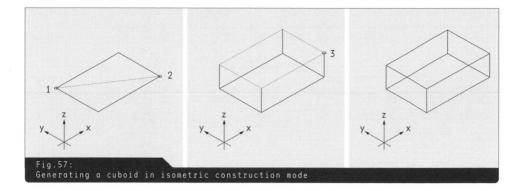

Fig.57:
Generating a cuboid in isometric construction mode

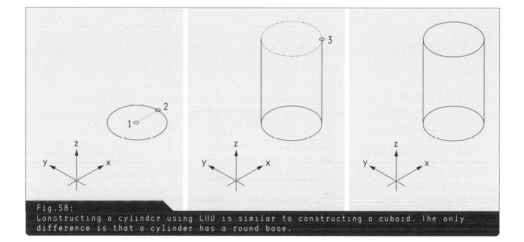

Fig.58:
Constructing a cylinder using CUD is similar to constructing a cuboid. The only difference is that a cylinder has a round base.

\\Tip:
In three-dimensional space, planes can be generated as polygon planes. In this case, you can use not only simple horizontal and vertical orientations but also any angle of inclination you require. If a plane is supposed to have a certain inclination, the simplest method is first to generate it in two dimensions in the top view and then to rotate it in three dimensions.

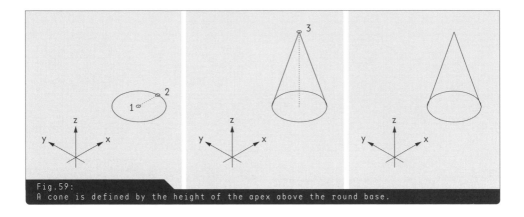

Fig.59:
A cone is defined by the height of the apex above the round base.

Cones

A cone is defined by a circular or elliptical base and narrows vertically to a point. When generating a cone, first define the base in terms of the base area and then determine the apex as a point using the Z axis.
> Fig. 59

Spheres

In CAD a sphere is defined using a midpoint in the base and a radius or diameter. The sphere's lines of latitude are positioned parallel to the XY plane of the UCS, and the vertical middle axis is congruent with the Z axis. > Fig. 60

Extruded volume bodies and planes

The 3D drawing functions described above make it very easy to generate simple geometric bodies with a single drawing command. Not all CAD programs offer these functions and in such cases the possibilities of geometric design are limited by preset form definitions. Another method of generating volume bodies is extrusion, which involves raising the body out of the ground plan sketch. This function allows you to transform two-dimensional objects consisting of lines, polylines and splines into volume bodies and planes.

This method is useful above all when working on objects that include rounded edges, bevels and other geometric peculiarities, since they are difficult to define without a preset basic shape. It is important that the figure consisting of line segments is closed and does not overlap with other figures. If the basic form is not closed, a plane is generated rather than a volume body.

Different CAD programs use different terms for extrusion, such as RAISE, TRANSLATION and TRAJECTION. Extrusion is carried out along a construction line or through entry of a height value. In the process of extrusion, the

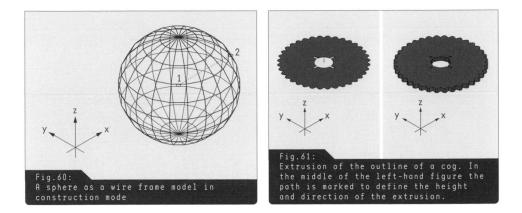

Fig.60:
A sphere as a wire frame model in
construction mode

Fig.61:
Extrusion of the outline of a cog. In
the middle of the left-hand figure the
path is marked to define the height
and direction of the extrusion.

two-dimensional basic shape that is to be transformed into a volume body is usually shown as an OUTLINE. The construction line along which the outline is to be extruded is often labelled PATH. Some CAD programs require both the basic shape and the three-dimensionally defined path in order to carry out the extrusion operation (e.g. Nemetschek Allplan). Others (e.g. Autodesk Architectural Desktop) need only a basic shape and a particular height, width and length entered as coordinates along the coordinate system axis in order to extrude a model from the outline. › Fig. 61

› Fig. 61

Rotational
solids

The ROTATION command enables you to rotate and generate a two-dimensional basic shape around the X or Y axis of the underlying UCS – or around any other axis defined by two points. As with the EXTRUSION command, ROTATION is particularly useful when dealing with objects with rounded edges and other details that are difficult or impossible to form using simple 3D drawing commands. Here, too, the outline of the underlying profile must be closed and cannot have any lines overlapping. In the

\\Tip:
Extruded volume bodies are very useful when generating terrain models. As in a cardboard model, where the terrain profile is reproduced in different layers, you can construct similar layers on the computer for every basic shape and extruded height and place them on top of one another.
Further information on manual modelbuilding can be found in *Basics Modelbuilding* by Alexander Schilling, Birkhäuser Publishers, Basel 2007.

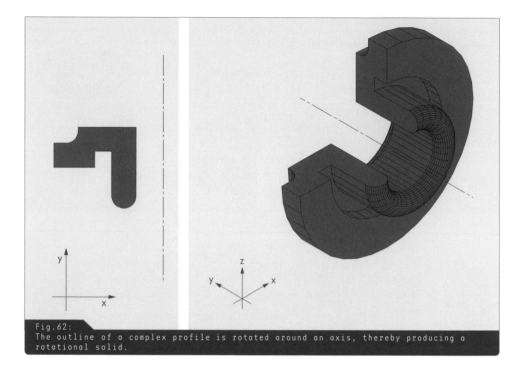

example provided in Figure 62, the profile positioned in the XY plane is rotated around an axis that is parallel to the Y axis of the UCS. The process is comparable to using a potting wheel that is spinning around a vertical axis, where the rotation makes it possible to form the modelling material to any shape you wish.

MODELLING

The previous chapters have presented construction methods that involve using a drawing function or deriving an outline to generate simple and complex volume bodies. Volume bodies can also be modelled, i.e. their fundamental shape can be altered. Depending on the geometry involved, one or more points of a body can be modified and moved in the directions prescribed by the axes of the UCS. For example, in only a few steps you can shape a cuboid into a wedge. › Fig. 63 Or – if you need to tackle a more complex operation – you can change the overall height of a building.

Construction
with volume
bodies

However, modelling is not restricted to simple manipulations of points. It can also be carried out in a large number of ways using com-

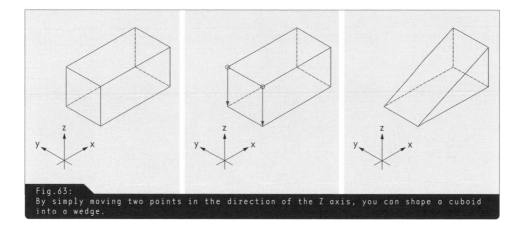

Fig.63:
By simply moving two points in the direction of the Z axis, you can shape a cuboid into a wedge.

mands that are at times more complex and at others quite simple. For example, the fact that volume bodies can be added to and subtracted from one another opens up a wide range of options. As with many drawing functions, these geometric operations go by different names in the various software packages, e.g. COMBINATION, CSG (short for Constructive Solid Geometry) and BOOLEAN OPERATIONS. The basic functions of these construction methods are based on addition, subtraction and intersection.

Addition
Addition allows you to combine two or more volume bodies into a single object. Here, the order in which the objects are selected for addition is unimportant. After they have been combined they can be selected and worked on only as a group, since they now constitute a newly defined object. This operation is particularly useful when separate building components need to be combined into a single structure. › Fig. 64b

Subtraction
Subtraction allows you to separate bodies from one another and to form different objects. In this operation the order of object activation is decisive, since only the first object to be activated remains intact while the second is erased along with the intersection volume. The second object thus determines the negative shape of the interpolation in the first. › Fig. 64c This operation makes it very easy, for example, to generate recesses for windows in wall components.

Intersections
When generating intersections, the intersection volume of two bodies is formed as a new object. The form of the object to be generated is determined by the way in which the two bodies are interpolated and is then shown as a positive shape. Areas that do not overlap are removed. › Fig. 64d

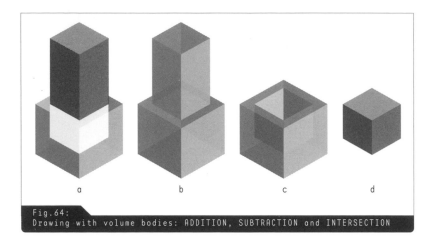

Fig.64:
Drawing with volume bodies: ADDITION, SUBTRACTION and INTERSECTION

ARCHITECTURAL ELEMENTS

Generally, CAD elements are defined geometrically or via the coordinates of their points. This geometric information allows the calculation of lengths, widths and heights and thus determines planes and volumes. In addition, it is possible to link this information to other specifications and to define general and specific characteristics. CAD programs that specialize in architectural drawing and visualization employ these associative possibilities for the efficient generation of typical architectural components. As a result, complex building components such as multi-layered walls, windows and stairs can largely be predefined and thus drawn with optimum accuracy. These components therefore no longer need to be constructed in many individual steps and subsequently combined; instead, they are predefined in a dialogue box. Moreover, depiction parameters for pens, hatching and the surfaces of a building component can be defined in terms of colour and transparency. › Chapter Visualization Furthermore, it is possible to prepare and categorize different building components for the subsequent calculation of planes and volumes. › Chapter TAI In this way an entire building can be efficiently constructed, visualized and quantified in virtual form.

Similarly to two-dimensional objects, architectural elements are usually constructed in the ground plan from the top view. The fundamental difference from 2D drawing is that you draw not simply a single line, but the entire component, creating several layers to record structure, height and the parameters for representing materials.

Drawing
architectural
elements

› 🖉

Walls

If you are drawing a wall as a complex component with a WALL tool, a dialogue box linked to the drawing function allows you to define the

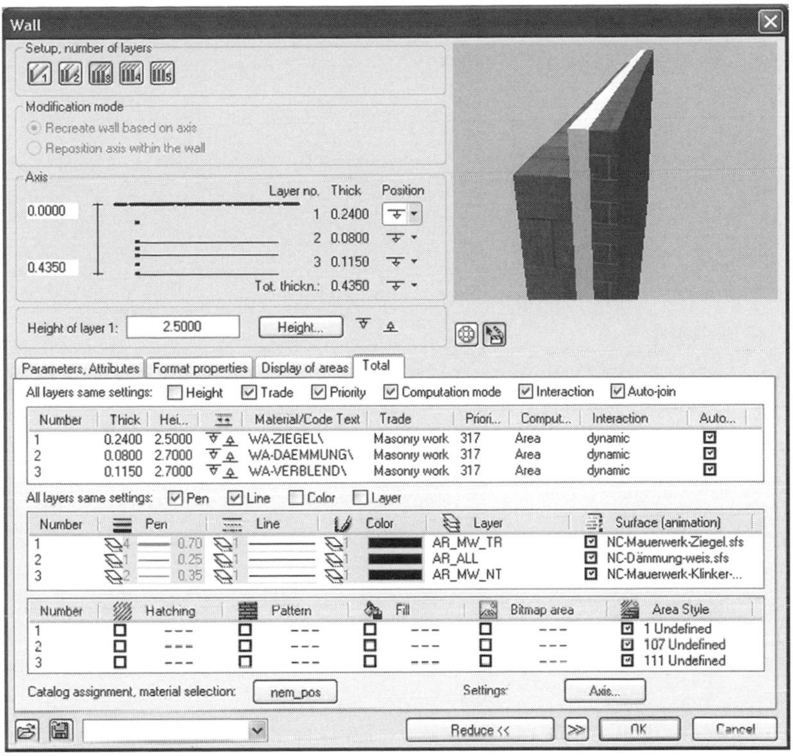

Fig.65:
Dialogue box for the WALL tool (Nemetschek Allplan)

characteristics of this component prior to the actual drawing process.
> Fig. 65

This means that you can set the default setting for wall height and structure to generate single or multi-layered elements. The layers are defined as lines with different pens and, if necessary, given additional at-

\\Hint:
An advantage of this type of design is the capacity to combine certain building components that associatively influence one another. For example, the material connections between two overlapping, multi-layered walls form automatically and do not require laborious design work.

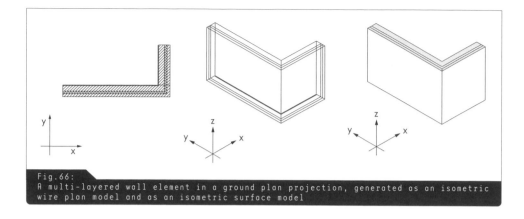

Fig.66:
A multi-layered wall element in a ground plan projection, generated as an isometric wire plan model and as an isometric surface model

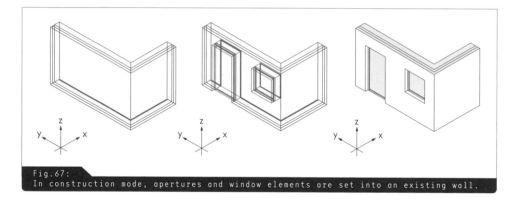

Fig.67:
In construction mode, apertures and window elements are set into an existing wall.

tributes that can be used for subsequent visualization or calculation of quantities. When you now draw the wall, the depiction will include all predefined information and the result will be a complex component. › Fig. 66 In this way a whole series of steps which are required when drawing 2D or even simple 3D elements are combined in a single drawing function.

Apertures, windows and doors

›

After you have drawn the walls as components, you can generate windows and doors in the wall planes in any format you choose. Rather than merely defining the width and height of an aperture, you can also insert and fit windows and doors as finished components with frames, partitions and panels. › Fig. 67

Ceilings

As in the automatic generation of walls, ceilings are defined geometrically in terms of shape, panel thickness and position, and are predefined in the depiction by means of hatching and surface characteristics.

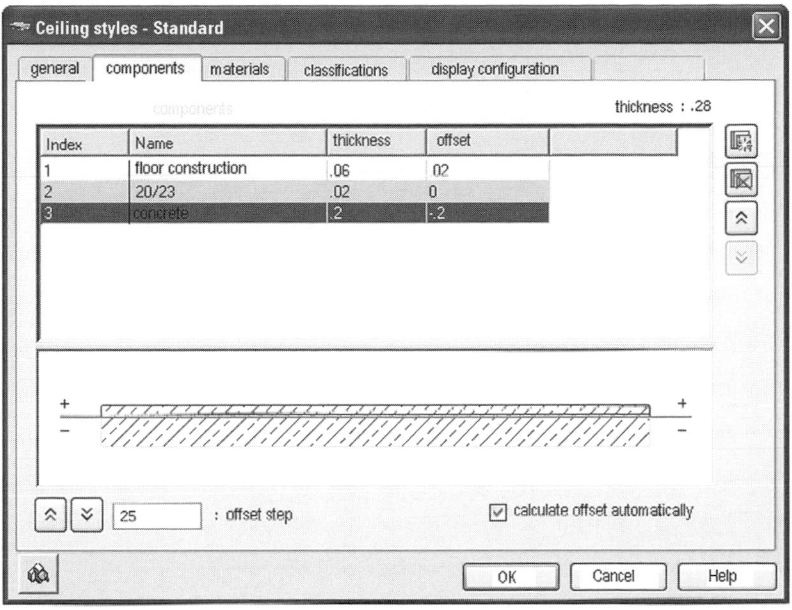

Fig. 68:
Dialogue box for CEILING tool (Autodesk Architectural Desktop)

If required, other attributes relating to the calculation of quantities and visualization can also be indicated. › Fig. 68

Once you have predefined the ceiling in this way, you can draw it with a base area of your choosing using a polyline and portray it as a completed component. Ceiling recesses such as stair openings can be constructed subsequently as polylines and recessed into the ceiling plane.

Stairs   When drawn by hand, stairs require laborious construction and calculation. CAD software combines the height and width of the stairs with

> \\Hint:
> Wall openings and inserted components such as
> doors and windows are associatively linked. The
> building components are automatically adapted
> to the structure of the wall with an appro-
> priate embrasure.

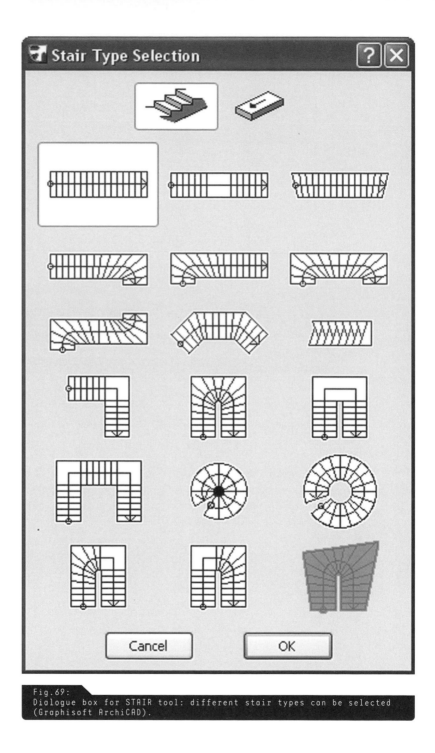

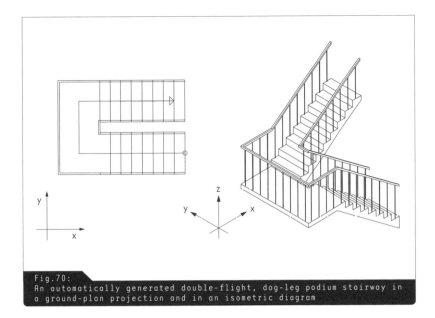

Fig.70:
An automatically generated double-flight, dog-leg podium stairway in
a ground-plan projection and in an isometric diagram

the stair ground plan and the height between floors to construct the stair
geometry, all of which parameters can be altered during or even after the
construction phase. Once you have selected the shape of the stairs, a dialogue box allows you to select and set their geometry and construction
details. › Fig. 69

The stairway and all its construction characteristics are automatically calculated and generated. They can then be checked in the three-
dimensional view and if necessary altered again. › Fig. 70

› ⓞ

ⓞ
\\Hint:
Some of the CAD programs that provide a stair
tool initially predefine the stairway as a
complete component in a dialogue box and allow
you to save it as a library element before you
place it within the virtual drawing area (e.g.
Graphisoft ArchiCAD.) Other programs use a predefined 2D ground plan as their basis, to which
you add geometric, constructive characteristics
by selecting polygonal points (e.g. Nemetschek
Allplan).

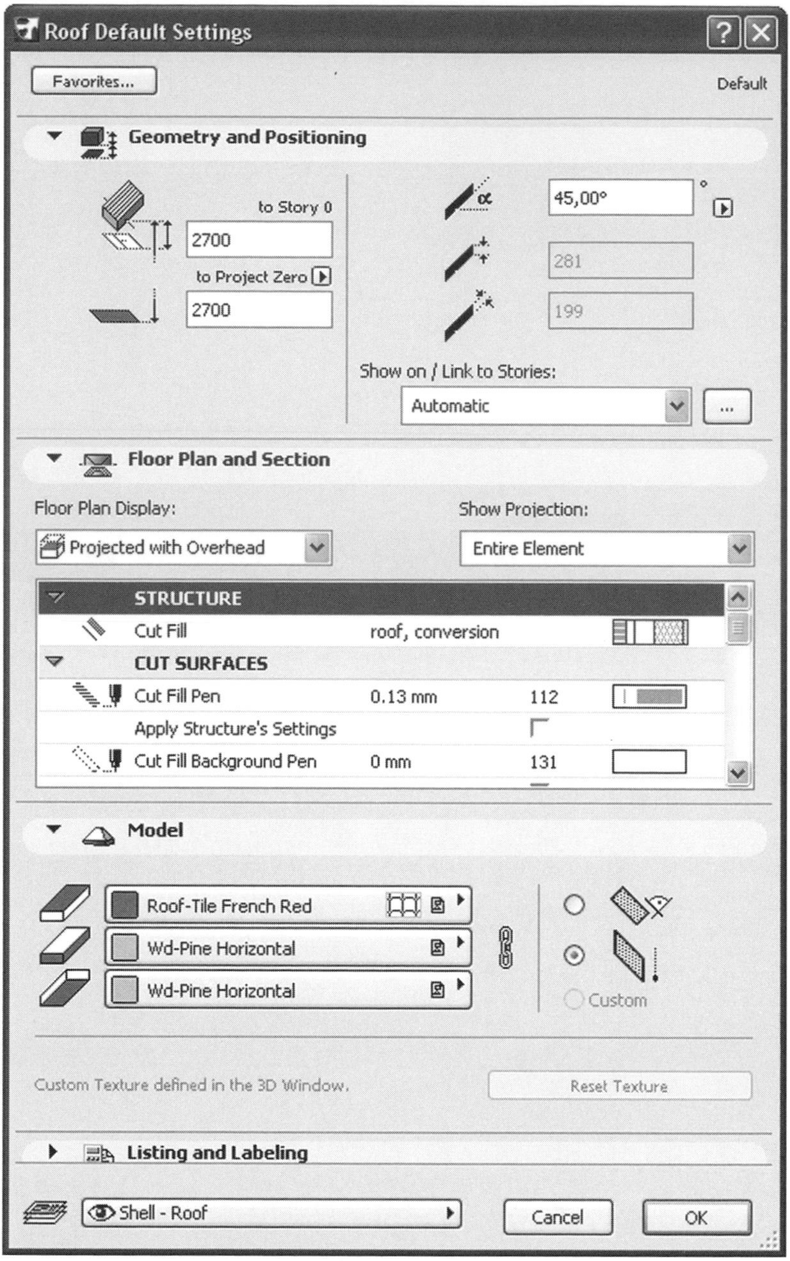
Roof Default Settings
Favorites...
Default
Geometry and Positioning
to Story 0
2700
to Project Zero
2700
45,00°
281
199
Show on / Link to Stories:
Automatic
Floor Plan and Section
Floor Plan Display:
Projected with Overhead
Show Projection:
Entire Element
STRUCTURE
Cut Fill
roof, conversion
CUT SURFACES
Cut Fill Pen
0.13 mm
112
Apply Structure's Settings
Cut Fill Background Pen
0 mm
131
Model
Roof-Tile French Red
Wd-Pine Horizontal
Wd-Pine Horizontal
Custom
Custom Texture defined in the 3D Window.
Reset Texture
Listing and Labeling
Shell - Roof
Cancel
OK

Fig.71:
Dialogue box for ROOF tool: along with line attributes, parameters can also be defined for storey height, roof inclination etc. (Graphisoft ArchiCAD).

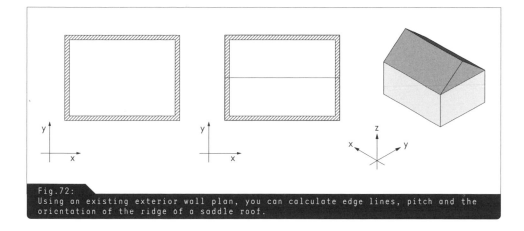

Fig.72:
Using an existing exterior wall plan, you can calculate edge lines, pitch and the orientation of the ridge of a saddle roof.

Roofs

Roofs are geometrically determined by the shape of the base area, the roof profile and inclination, the ridge, the edge height, and in some cases by the overhang. In many CAD systems, simple roofs can be designed with a ROOF tool by drawing the base area of the roof as a polyline and entering all desired parameters of the roof profile using the corresponding dialogue box. › Figs 71 and 72

\\Tip:
Once the shape of the roof has been generated, many CAD programs allow you almost automatically to generate a rafter plan and definitions of the roof structure. These programs are thus able to take a virtual model from the design stage to the construction planning stage in only a few steps.

VISUALIZATION

In architecture, the term visualization refers to the pictorial representation of a detail or a planned building. One of the advantages of computer simulation over technical drawing as a means of visualization is that computer imaging is easier for non-professionals – including many building clients – to comprehend, because it provides a visual translation of the technical information contained in a construction drawing.

Visualization –
a design tool

Computer visualizations serve different purposes. Planners can use them as a design tool to check the proportions of structural elements and spatial relationships between components and their surroundings.

Fig. 73:
Visualization as a design tool: cubatures, lighting and materials can be examined in different phases of the design process.

In addition, visualizations can be used to evaluate the effects of various materials and lighting conditions when planning building projects. Using simple and relatively abstract virtual models at an early stage in the design process, you can check many aspects of the design, such as the suitability of materials and structural proportions. You can thus generate detailed computer simulations that, depending on the stage of the design and the degree of differentiation incorporated into the original virtual model, can help you make decisions during the planning process. The possibilities open to you range from simple mass models to virtual buildings, which reflect the current stage of planning. > Fig. 73

Computer visualizations also enable you to evaluate the advantages and disadvantages of different design approaches in the context of the planned location. While the exterior space remains unchanged, you can examine the relationship between the different architectural languages of alternative structures and the location. > Fig. 74

> ✎

Visualization
for
presentation

Architectural visualizations – like other methods of representation such as drawings and scale models can also be used for the final presentation of a design. Depending on the requirements of the specific design and the target group, a visualization can be photorealistic or abstract. A successful presentation need not necessarily use photorealistic depictions: simple cubatures and abstracted surfaces can be non-realistic yet still communicate many aspects of the envisioned architectural effect. > Fig. 75

If possible, virtual models should be constructed to reflect subsequent visualizations. It is an advantage to adapt the degree of detail in a model to the possibilities of the visual presentation in order to use time efficiently in both the design and computation of a visualization. > Chapters

📎

\\Hint:
In order to generate a visualization you need appropriate software, called rendering software (see Chapter Rendering parameters and Appendix, Table 4). A number of CAD programs include an integrated rendering module that executes at least the initial steps in the visualization process. To achieve good, detailed results, you will often need special software, referred to as a renderer.

✎

\\Tip:
Many rendering programs allow you to position a pixel image in the background of a virtual object and thus to create a real backdrop in a virtual situation. For example, by using a digital photo of surrounding structures as a background image, you can depict a planned building in its actual future surroundings.

Fig.74:
Different architectural approaches in the same urban-planning
context

Three-dimensional design and Rendering parameters For instance, details such as protuberances, recesses, window allocations and the exact differentiation of materials are not necessary for the simulated aerial view of an urban design, because they cannot be seen from a great distance. › Fig. 76

It is only at closer distances that details of the building cubatures and the structure of materials become visible and thereby important for the visualization. Features of the external space such as trees, cars and people can also fill a visualization with life, creating – as in a photo –

Fig.75:
Abstract visualizations can clarify many aspects of a design.

Fig.76:
Visualization of a planned urban structure

Fig.77:
The details of a building and its surrounding become more important as the viewer draws closer.

familiar references to everyday life and providing the viewer with a means to grasp the scale of the objects being depicted. › Fig. 77

Interior space also plays an important role in architectural visualizations. When creating a realistic interior visualization, you should pay attention to structural details and surface qualities, since interior views are often presented in close-up. › Fig. 78

SURFACES

An important part of a computer visualization is the optical effect of surfaces, which are given their material quality by colours, textures and lighting effects.

\\Tip:
In a visualization of a high technical quality, virtual worlds seem perfect — and precisely for this reason unrealistic. The real world contains many "mistakes" that are significant for a computer visualization. Creating virtual façades with slightly uneven surfaces and colour nuances, for example, produces a better visualization with a much more realistic effect.

Colours   In the real world, it is the colour spectrum that allows us to perceive surfaces visually. The light that hits a surface is absorbed or reflected. If the entire colour spectrum is reflected by an object it appears white; if the entire colour spectrum is absorbed it appears black. Thus, our perception

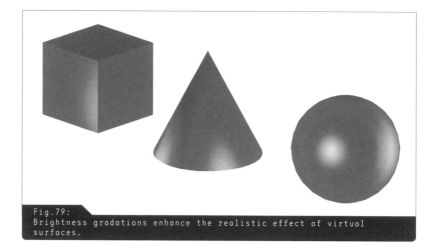

Fig.79:
Brightness gradations enhance the realistic effect of virtual surfaces.

of a colour depends on whether it is reflected or absorbed by the surface. For example, a blue surface reflects the colour blue while absorbing all other colour values.

An important method for creating realistic simulations of surfaces is selectively to change their colours. To have a realistic effect, the colour values of objects need to show nuances that are produced by differences in the way they reflect light. › Fig. 79

The sides that are turned away from the light source appear darker than those directly exposed to it. Moreover, highlights on strongly reflective surfaces appear white, irrespective of the colour of the object. As a rule, the possibilities for defining the rendered objects offered by the rendering software allow you to introduce variations in both the surface colour and the reflected colour, as well as in specific mirroring and transparency characteristics. If required, these can be set as percentages in a dialogue box.

You can use the electronic pen with which you drew the object to define its colour properties and reflective and transparency characteristics. Within the CAD system, the pen, or pen colour, is associated with the corresponding virtual information that is represented in the computer visualization as visible characteristics. › Chapter The virtual drawing board

Textures

Textures can be applied to the surfaces of a virtual object in order to represent a wide range of materials. This usually involves using a detail of

Fig.80:
Textures can be used for the visualization of surfaces in a rendering.

a <u>pixel image</u> – e.g. a photographic close-up of a brick wall. › Chapter Rendering parameters With the help of the so-called MAPPING function, you can place this pixel image on the virtual surface and adapt the textured area to the size you require. Finally, when the view of the texture – in this case, a virtual brick wall – is rendered, it has the same surface of its real correlate. This is how a piece of the real world is imported via a photo to the virtual model and used for the visualization. › Fig. 80

LIGHT AND SHADE

Well-placed light sources and selectively applied shadow effects are important for creating realistic surfaces and a particular atmosphere. Rendering software enables you to position and adjust different virtual light sources to simulate lighting conditions in exterior and interior space.

Virtual light sources

Virtual light sources can be used with differing intensities and colours. Moreover, it is possible to make light visible that under normal conditions is invisible until it falls on a surface – an effect that is similar to the light from a torch shining through fog.

\\ Example:
While a normal window glass is transparent, it also reflects the surroundings to a certain degree. As a rule, you can check the effect of the settings for the respective surface materials in a renderer preview. Given a little practice with the software, you will thus be able to carry out the initial stages of simulating the object you have in mind.

\\ Tip:
As a rule, a selection of standardized textures is provided by the rendering software. This means that you can try out some initial textures without having to photograph the environment you are dealing with. In addition, you can find a large selection by running a search on the keyword "texture" on the Internet.

Fig.81:
Light sources have a great influence on the atmosphere of a visualization.

Fig.82:
A spotlight is a directional light source emitting light that spreads out in a cone. Depending on the angle at which the light falls on the surface, the target point is enclosed by a circle or an ellipse.

Fig.83:
A parallel light emits a directional shaft of light that does not form a cone.

Fig.84:
A point light emits non-directional light that spreads out in the space like the illumination from a light bulb.

Spotlight, parallel light and point light are different virtual light sources that create distinctive light distributions and effects. › Figs 81–84

Ambient light   Apart from local light sources, ambient light can also be used in a design. This non-directional light is distributed equally throughout a space and constantly illuminates and colours the objects within this space. The brighter this light, the weaker the influence of other sources of illumination. You should use ambient light to fine-tune lighting and to avoid saturation or clouding in the visualization.

Intensity of illumination

The intensity of illumination is controlled via the colour of light, which is set individually for each light source in a scene. The brighter the colour, the stronger the luminosity of the light source. Pure white has the greatest luminosity. If you find that the luminosity of a light source is not sufficient, you can activate additional light sources. Since light colours can have all the colour values of the light colour spectrum, they can illuminate the space in every possible colour.

Shadows

Like real light sources, virtual light sources can produce shadows, thereby enhancing the realism of a virtual scene. Different methods of computing shadows can be used to produce hard, soft and area shadows.
> Figs 85–87

PERSPECTIVE AND VIRTUAL CAMERA

The choice of the right perspective is key to computer visualization.
> Figs 73–78 All factors relevant to the image should be taken up in an appealing image format, if necessary with striking details. Image content should also be shown at a normal angle so that viewers will find parallels to the real world in the use of perspective. During the visualization process, you can arrange elements of a virtual model in combination with virtual light sources from an advantageous perspective. These form the render scene.

\\Hint:
Although sunlight should generally be understood as point light, it has an effect similar to parallel light when it strikes the Earth's surface due to the sun's enormous size.

\\Tip:
Some CAD programs include sun and shadow studies as a design aid (e. g. Graphisoft ArchiCAD and Nemetschek Allplan). To set the position of the sun, you enter into a dialogue box the desired latitude, longitude, time of day and time of the year. This allows you to simulate the lighting conditions in any place on Earth at any time and thus provides you with valuable information on the effects of building orientation.

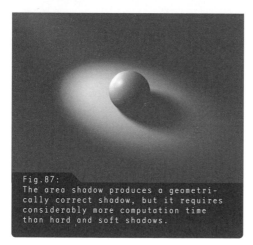

Fig.85:
The light source produces a hard
shadow which, while not geometrically
precise, requires little computation
time.

Fig.86:
This soft shadow appears more realistic than the hard shadow in Fig. 85
and can be computed as a greyscale
graphic in a relatively short time.

Fig.87:
The area shadow produces a geometrically correct shadow, but it requires
considerably more computation time
than hard and soft shadows.

The use of scenes often saves time because they can be stored as a template and thus do not have to be recreated for every visualization computation. As a rule, the render scene is visualized using a virtual camera, which can be used and adjusted within the application parameters like a real camera and defines <u>eyepoint</u>, <u>aiming point</u>, <u>focal distance</u> and <u>camera angle</u>. › Fig. 88 The eyepoint corresponds to the "eye level" of the observer in the virtual space. Like the aiming point of the view, it can be defined via coordinates in three dimensions. › Chapter Coordinate systems

🗍

\\Hint:
When using rendering software, you can generally store scenes and retrieve them at a later
point. A scene is an arrangement of virtual
objects and light sources shown from a selected
perspective that can normally be adjusted by
means of virtual cameras (see Chapter Perspective and virtual camera).

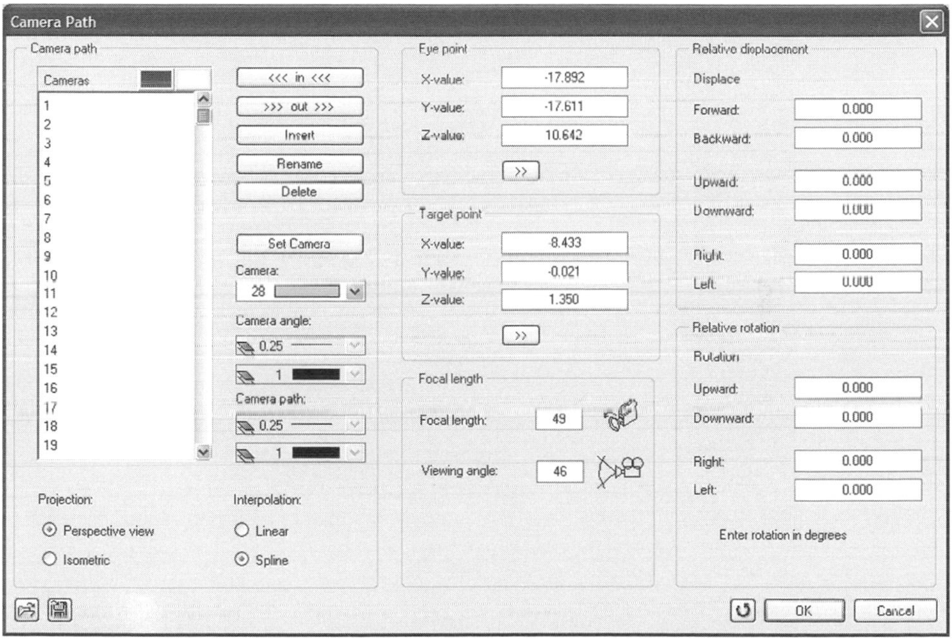

Fig.88:
Setting options for the parameters of a virtual camera (Nemetschek Allplan)

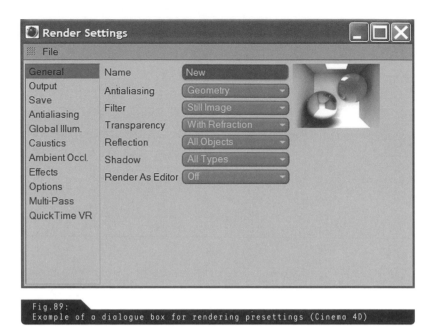

Fig.89:
Example of a dialogue box for rendering presettings (Cinema 4D)

The camera angle and the focal distance are geometrically dependent on each other and determine the visible field of the camera perspective: reducing the focal distance allows you to extend the visible field even in cramped spatial situations. However, to avoid the "fisheye" effect, you should not reduce the focal distance too much. If possible, eyepoint and aiming point should be located at the same height so that vertical edges can be depicted parallel to one another.

\\Hint:
Many rendering programs offer a variety of
rendering engines (rendering types) that
differ in terms of their basic computational
methods. They include Raytracing, Phong
Shading, Gouraud Shading, OpenGL and Z-Buffer.
A simple way to compare image quality, calculation times and the advantages/disadvantages
of each engine is to generate renderings of
the same object.

RENDERING PARAMETERS

The quality of a visualization is based not only on an optimum arrangement of objects, surfaces and light sources, but also on the technical quality of the image. This quality depends on a wide variety of parameters, which must be properly harmonized. One method of defining parameters is by the presettings of the rendering software. We provide a basic explanation of these parameters below. > Fig. 89

Generally speaking, the term "rendering" refers to the generation of new data from suitable "raw" or source data. In the specialized field of computer visualization, it describes the process of converting a <u>vector graphic</u> into a <u>bit-mapped graphic</u>.

Resolution The resolution of a pixel graphic is based on the number of pixels in a given area and determines the quality of the image. Normally, resolution is expressed by the abbreviation <u>dpi</u> (dots per inch) as the width x height of the image. The more pixels there are in an image, the finer the resolution. Conversely, an image with fewer pixels looks grainier and the depiction of finer details is not as crisp. > Fig. 90

In conjunction with the total number of pixels, the resolution determines the effective size of a pixel graphic as expressed in centimetres. At a resolution of 300 dpi, a 1000 × 1000 pixel rendering has a square shape measuring 8.47 cm × 8.47 cm. If the resolution is reduced to 150 dpi, the size of the image increases significantly to 16.94 cm × 16.94 cm, and the same number of pixels is distributed over an area that is four times as large. This is why, in contrast to a vector graphic, a pixel graphic cannot be enlarged without a loss of quality, since only the size of the individual dots increases. This affects the quality of the image, which becomes "pixelated" and has a coarser resolution.

\\Hint:
A vector graphic is a two- or three-dimensional computer image composed of different drawn elements, each of which is defined by coordinates. In contrast to bit-mapped graphics (see below), vector graphics can be enlarged to any desired size without a loss of quality. Compared to other graphics formats, they also require little memory volume.

\\Hint:
Bit-mapped graphics (also called pixel graphics) consist of an arrangement of individual pixels. A pixel is the smallest unit of a pixel graphic and contains a particular colour value as graphic information. Put differently, a pixel graphic is a combination of many pixels that is comparable to a mosaic of many small elements.

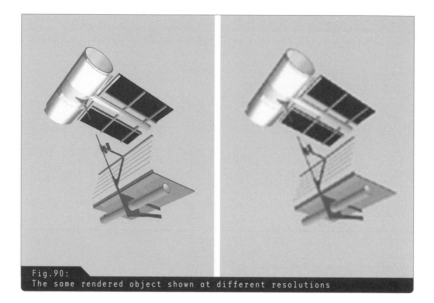

Fig.90:
The same rendered object shown at different resolutions

You need only a little experience to determine the required computational times based on the planned resolution of a rendering. If a larger
number of pixels need to be calculated for a computer graphic, the calculation will require more time and effort. Renderings that represent inter-
mediary stages of the design generally require a lower resolution than
final presentations and their rendering times will be shorter too.

Anti-aliasing

When converting a vector graphic to a pixel graphic, you can use
anti-aliasing to avoid a jagged depiction of diagonal lines (the so-called
stair effect). A pixel graphic is only capable of portraying horizontal and
vertical lines without great difficulty. If a line is slanted, "stairs" appear
because slanted lines are portrayed by offset square pixels in a pixel
graphic. › Fig. 91

The same effect can be seen in all kinds of round shapes and even
in typefaces. The grainier the resolution, the larger will be the individual
pixels – and the more pronounced the stair effect. Anti-aliasing interpolates and partially weakens the colour values of the individual "steps" so
that they are not as distinct. The level of anti-aliasing has a substantial
effect on the time needed to compute a rendering: if the round shapes
and diagonal lines need to be portrayed crisply, the calculation will take
longer. This is why maximum anti-aliasing should only be used for final
presentations.

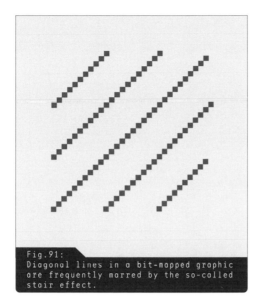

Fig.91:
Diagonal lines in a bit-mapped graphic
are frequently marred by the so-called
stair effect.

Aside from the wealth of geometric information required for a virtual model, the rendering settings, in particular, exert a great influence on the time needed to compute a visualization. For this reason you should, if possible, consider the purpose and the intended quality of a visualization or rendering result before you begin the rendering process. > Appendix, Table 2

\\Tip:
You can also increase resolution to diminish the stair effect. In this case, the diagonal lines and edges are calculated using an especially large number of pixels and there is a finer depiction of the inevitable jagged patterns.

\\Tip:
You should first test the rendering settings on a detail from the virtual scene in order to examine, in advance, the effects of light and materials. Complex models, in particular, may require a rendering time of several hours.

PROGRAM LIBRARIES

CAD programs normally feature integrated program libraries with an array of symbols, document templates and predefined building components. Architectural CAD programs include sundry objects that can serve as standard drawing elements or that can be changed to reflect your own style and ideas. > Fig. 92

You can also create templates from objects you have drawn yourself and use them in more than one project. It will save you a great deal of time to use objects defined in this way since no intensive research is required; and you can integrate objects into drawings, and copy and edit them as you require, instead of drawing them from scratch in the future.

Symbols

There are symbols to represent both interior furnishings (furniture, bathroom fittings, kitchen elements etc.) and elements of landscape design (trees, plants, cars, people etc.). Additional icons depict objects in the field of structural engineering, building services technology and the planning disciplines linked to architecture.

Building components

The use of standardized components saves a great deal of work, particularly when you create working drawings, because you can then select drawing elements like steel components (beams, pipes etc.) and connectors (screws, bolts etc.) from a catalogue, incorporate them directly into the drawing and edit them there. Even complex components such as stairways, windows and doors can be stored and used in this way. > Chapter Architectural elements

Pixel images

In addition to elements in vector graphics, pixel images can also be incorporated into libraries and administered there. These images may

\\Tip:
Using a scanner, you can scan both freehand sketches and other hand-drawn technical drawings, and then import them as pixel graphics into CAD drawings. Conversely, you may also print out mid-project CAD drawings, modify them by hand using transparent paper, and then transpose the results to CAD. This is one way to combine the advantages of CAD and hand drawings.

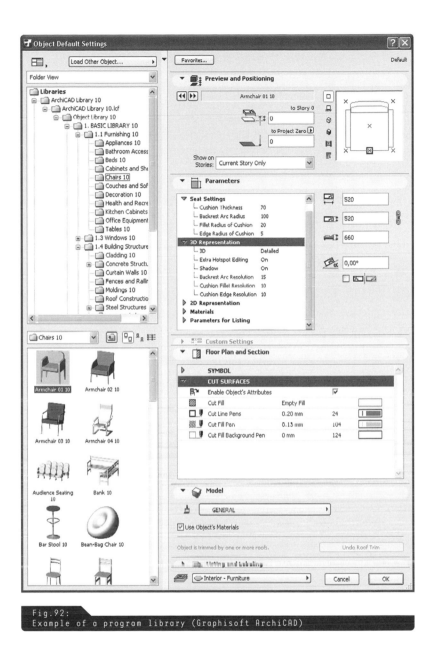

Fig.92:
Example of a program library (Graphisoft ArchiCAD)

include digital photographs, scans and renderings that are systematically imported, stored, and – if needed – integrated into a drawing.

Drawing frames can also be imported and edited, and the same applies to standardized lettering and drawing headers in the respective scale. This means you need to create customized document and printing templates only once. These are then stored for later use in the program library.

> Chapter Printing and plotting

CAD INTERFACES

CAD interfaces facilitate the exchange of data between different programs. Although all CAD systems generally work with vector graphic information, most programs employ their own file formats, which are often incompatible and impede data exchange between different CAD programs. DXF has largely caught on as the standard data exchange format for architectural drawings, as it can be read and written by nearly all CAD software and even by a few graphics programs.

DXF is short for <u>drawing interchange format</u> (or drawing exchange format) and was developed by the company Autodesk to exchange CAD data.

If a DXF file is imported into a CAD program, different options can be chosen to adapt specific properties of the vector graphic data. These include unit, scale and the two- or three-dimensional mode of transmission. > Fig. 93

A number of architectural CAD programs not only use DXF and their own data formats, but also provide interfaces to select programs in order to ensure trouble-free data exchanges. This is particularly true in the field of rendering programs – the additional software necessary to guarantee outstanding visualization results. For instance, Nemetschek Allplan uses a special data format to export three-dimensional models to Cinema 4D rendering software, Autodesk Architectural Desktop offers a comparable

\\Hint:
Exchanging different CAD data is not unproblematic and rarely goes off perfectly. Important details specific to a CAD system are often lost or may not be displayed in the same way as the original exported information. This can become glaringly evident in the case of typefaces, program-specific symbols and dimensioning data, since they rarely have an equivalent in the target system.

\\Hint:
Special programs that read and write data in several file formats and thus facilitate imports and exports between different CAD programs provide an alternative to DXF-based data exchanges. That said, you may have difficulty transmitting data if you lack the necessary experience.

interface to 3D STUDIO MAX/VIZ, and Graphisoft ArchiCAD has developed an interface for Artlantis.

TAI

TAI, short for tendering, awarding and invoicing, represents an important area of building construction. After architects create the design and construction documentation for an architectural object, bids or tenders are invited for the individual construction jobs – in other words, this work is described in written form, its scope is specified, and this information is made available to construction companies together with relevant drawings so they can submit a tender. After a quotation is received, the construction company is selected based on the specified prices and quality standards, and the construction work is commissioned. Finally, after the construction work is completed, accounts must be settled for the costs incurred.

Special tendering, awarding and invoicing programs make it easier to manage quantities and costs in building construction. When architects create a structure as a complete virtual model using CAD, they can categorize the quantities of the individual building components according to materials and skilled trades. › Chapter **Architectural elements** This information can be imported directly to the TAI programs and edited there, eliminating the need for time-consuming calculations of quantities by hand.

From the CAD system to TAI software to the construction site and back again

Ideally, data will flow from the CAD drawing to the tendering program. Setting quantities links components from the CAD drawing directly to the TAI program, allowing users to check the allocation, quantities and dimensions of components and items in both the CAD and the TAI system. This allows you to compile a list of contract specifications efficiently and monitor their completion effectively. Information from the CAD program (attributes, quantities etc.) can be calculated and organized in corresponding lists.

PRINTING AND PLOTTING

› 🗋

› ✎

After a drawing is completed in design mode, it can be printed or plotted. While large-size CAD drawings are printed on plotters, small formats are printed on standard DIN A4 and A3 printers.

Drawings and plans are usually prepared for printing in special windows that allow you to arrange different drawing content and pixel images on a page, as well as subsequently labelling them and making other settings relevant to printing.

Print scale

Here you make the final specifications regarding the printing scale and the required paper size. You also have an additional opportunity to examine, prior to printing, the effect of scale-related settings such as line

🗋

\\Hint:
Plotters are large-format printers, usually DIN A1 or A0, on which plans are printed on roll paper. Roll widths normally measure 61.5 cm for A1 rolls and 91.5 cm for A0 rolls. Plan sizes can be entered individually into the CAD programs so that every plan format can be used inside the given roll width.

✎

\\Tip:
When printing on a plotter, you can usually choose from three different quality settings. A low quality level will print much more quickly than a higher setting, but the print will have a lower resolution and not be as sharp. Lower settings also use less ink.

width and font size. In this context it is important to make sure that the reference scale matches the printing scale, since characters and other scale-dependent features of a drawing might otherwise be too small or too large. › Chapter The virtual drawing board

For instance, if a plan is supposed to show a façade section together with corresponding detail views, it is possible to present drawings in different scales on a single architectural plan. In this case, each individual drawing is depicted in the required scale.

› 🗋

Paper formats

Plan formats with different aspect ratios are available for presentation purposes. It usually makes sense to choose a common paper format for architectural drawings (e.g. the ISO/DIN A series), since it is easy to produce them. Large formats are needed for construction drawings, while for case of detail drawings, it is generally better to use a format that can be copied on most copy machines, such as DIN A3 or A4.

A drawing frame created for the selected paper format generally defines the area taken up by the drawing, and shows the edge that can be used to subsequently cut the drawing. The drawing header contains technical information such as a precise description of the content (floor plan, section, view etc.), the scale (M 1:50, 1:100, 1:100 etc.), as well as printing date, author and other supplementary data. › Fig. 94

The drawing frame and header can be created as templates in the required scale, making it possible to use the basic settings for other projects as well. › Chapter Program libraries

Virtual print

You can also print drawings and plans "virtually" in the form of files. In this case, you do not transmit the vector graphic information in a drawing to a real printer or plotter but store it as a plot file using the printer software. A plot file contains all the drawing information that is required

---

🗋

\\Hint:
There are sometimes significant differences in the plan design options provided by CAD programs, and their ease of use can differ too. A few providers offer supplementary modules specially developed for plan design and printout (e.g. Nemetschek Plandesign).

✎

\\Tip:
This method can be employed in a number of situations — for example, if a student does not own a plotter and needs to make a print on the university's plotter or at a professional copy shop. Data can be printed on the plotter without installing the corresponding CAD program on the attached computer.

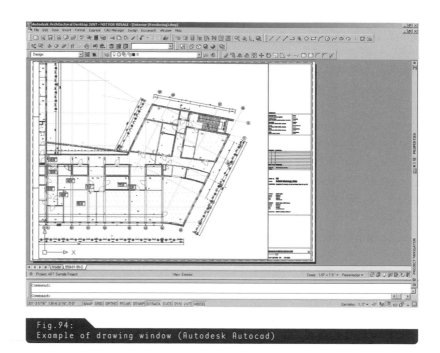

by a specific printer or plotter to print out the drawing at a subsequent point in time without using the CAD software's printing environment.

PDF

PDF stands for "portable document format" and is a common data exchange format developed by Adobe Systems that can contain both vector graphic and bit-mapped information. Many CAD systems allow you to create PDF files as an export function. Alternatively, you can install a virtual printer (e.g. Adobe Acrobat Distiller) in much the same way as a real printer and then select it for printing. It will create a PDF document containing all the graphic information of the virtually printed drawing.

Pixel graphics

A few CAD systems allow you to export drawing content as pixel graphics. These can be stored both in different file formats and, if required, in user-defined resolutions, two examples being the JPEG or/and TIFF formats. A distinguishing feature of the JPEG format is that the bit-mapped graphic information is mostly stored in compressed form so the file sizes are accordingly small and easy to manage. The TIFF format requires much more memory, but it contains a great deal more graphic information and is better suited for additional editing steps (e.g. image-editing programs).

SYSTEM REQUIREMENTS

HARDWARE
Even though, as the user of a computer, you do not necessarily need to know much about its inner workings, we are including the following sections to provide some basic information about a number of hardware components.

Central processing unit

The central processing unit, or CPU, is the heart of the computer and controls all its other components.

Mainboard

The mainboard (also known as "motherboard") is the central circuit board of the computer and has attachment points for its processor and memory modules as well as for supplementary cards such as graphics, sound and network cards. These components can also be integrated directly into the mainboard, in which case they are said to be "onboard."

RAM – working memory

RAM, short for random access memory, is your computer's working memory.

Graphics card

The graphics card in a PC controls the screen display, ensuring, among other things, that data are computed quickly for visualizations. For CAD systems, it is advisable not to have an onboard graphics card since the relatively slow RAM will be used for graphics processing and the other processes may be slowed down.

Hard drive

A hard drive is a storage medium that writes data on the magnetic surface of a rotating disc. The surface is magnetized based on the information being recorded. Even if a hard drive has sufficient memory capacity for all CAD data and is a relatively secure storage device, you should regularly secure CAD data on external media such as CDs and DVDs to protect against possible data loss.

Monitor

The screen size of a monitor is normally indicated in inches and is based on the screen diagonal. The screen should not be too small since it is used to display the virtual workspace. Alternatively, you can use two screens: if you display all the interface's control functions on one, you can use the virtual drawing area on the other without restriction. Please keep in mind, though, that your graphics card must support this setup.

Special input devices

Aside from the keyboard and the mouse, other input devices have been specially designed for the virtual workspace. The best-known are the joysticks used to play three-dimensional computer games.

The SpaceMouse functions like a joystick and can efficiently control virtual views. Additional keys can be programmed to execute drawing and tool commands.

Sketchpad

The sketchpad, also called a "digitizing board," digitizes data entered with a pen-like pointing device. Since the sketchpad provides a much higher resolution than a standard computer mouse, you can use it to draw an object in much the same way as you would draw on a piece of paper with a pencil. When assigned the appropriate scale, the drawing area of the user interface will correspond to that of the sketchpad.

Touchscreen

New touchscreens can also be used for drawing, like sketchpads. The touchscreen is not set up vertically like a monitor in front of the user, but is used as a horizontal work surface to create and display drawings.

SOFTWARE

If at all possible, you should choose CAD software to match existing hardware. The use of modern software on old computing systems can be problematic, since these may not provide the computational capacity required to execute the software operations adequately. You must also have a suitable <u>operating system</u>, which controls the computer's fundamental processes. This is a basic requirement for running all application software. The most popular operating systems are Windows (Microsoft), Mac OS (Apple) and, increasingly, LINUX, which you can largely use without a license. Not all operating systems are suitable for all CAD systems, and you should pay close attention to the software providers' specifications.

There is a large selection of CAD software on the market, and the various CAD programs often function differently and have significant price differences. From freeware and shareware to costly specialized programs, the offerings are immense. › Appendix, Table 3

An alternative to the expensive complete versions of CAD software are the demo and student versions that a few providers make available to consumers. The student versions are inexpensive compared to the normal versions, and you can even use the demo versions for free for a limited period. Even so, it is prohibited to use them professionally. A demo version may make sense to take the first few steps with CAD since it allows you to try out the software and evaluate its strengths and weaknesses.

Selecting software

Selecting a CAD system depends on a number of factors: the (architecturally relevant) functions, the special properties of operation and use, the cost and the required hardware. An additional criterion is the CAD user's personal or professional environment since data exchange with project partners – to name just one example – should be as trouble-free as possible and is best ensured by exchanging data from one and the same software program.

Program-specific literature is available for the various CAD programs in addition to training courses at universities, adult education centres and private institutions. If you do not want to learn CAD on your own – which is, of course, entirely possible – you can take a course that suits your particular level of expertise.

It is advantageous to learn not just a single CAD system, but to master at least the basic principles of other programs so that you are not restricted to particular system requirements and remain flexible in your work. Although the operation of many CAD programs differs, they all have the same underlying foundations. Once you have a good command of these basics, you can apply this knowledge to other programs and learn them more easily.

\\Hint:
Different software providers will make recommendations concerning hardware configurations. These should be regarded as minimum requirements when you purchase your CAD system. The software may function on the recommended hardware, but it may not be able to carry out work processes involving large volumes of data. This is why it is worthwhile to get advice from a specialized vendor on which computer system to buy.

\\Tip:
Freeware and shareware can be downloaded from the Internet but in most cases only offer limited basic functionality.

DESIGNING IN DIALOGUE WITH THE COMPUTER

The computer in general and drawing with CAD in particular stream-line work processes and provide a basis for efficient and exact approaches to creating and managing digital drawings and other data. Associative components and virtual models not only simulate reality, but also influence it directly by offering a new manner of designing and systematized planning process. But even with all its benefits, this working method has a few drawbacks. Designing with CAD usually entails drawing with a mouse, which cannot be guided as precisely as a pencil. Also, you only have indirect contact with the drawn object via the entry and output devices—an aspect of the work that should never be underestimated. When drawing with CAD, beginners, in particular, are confronted with many operations that may initially seem complicated and can influence their mental processes, particularly when they engage in creative design.

By contrast, drawing by hand is often an intuitive process in which personal ideas are implemented directly and sometimes even largely unconsciously. The results on paper are continually influenced while you draw, and the representational method, which is, not least, dependent on experience and feel, is aligned with the drawing material and the represented object. This is another reason that you should incorporate hand drawings into the design process and, if possible, enhance the use of the CAD application with hand sketches.

Outlook   CAD has become a firm feature of the day-to-day work of designers, and it will continue to grow in importance in the future. In the field of architecture, the developments playing an especially important role are those that allow all project participants to have direct access to an object as a virtual model – from the creation of the design and working drawings to the construction of the object. This makes it possible to evaluate, print and even modify the data and drawings that are relevant to planning and construction directly. It lays a foundation for virtual planning that is always up to date and, if need be, reflects the architectural object down to the finest detail. In addition, even when it accompanies an ongoing development process, CAD influences the development of new approaches to planning and allows for the design of architectural structures that could not completely be depicted by hand drawings, including amorphous and other free forms. In this context, complex structural calculations or the computation of complicated component geometries are an important basis for the design and construction process. CAD represents much more than an easy-to-use drawing tool. It is both a comprehensive instrument and an important building block in the development and future of architecture.

APPENDIX

CHECKLISTS AND OVERVIEW OF SOFTWARE

Table 1: Sample layer structure for designing a building

Environment	Building
	Development
	Trees
	Piece of property
Design	Design grid
	Layouts
	Views
	Sections
Loadbearing structure	Construction grid
	Foundations
	Exterior walls
	Interior walls
	Columns
	Beams
	Stairs
	Ceilings
	Roof structure
Building finishing	Grid
	Lightweight construction
	Electrical installation
	Heating and plumbing
Furnishings	Bathroom fixtures
	Furniture
	Objects
	Flooring

Drawing information	Dimensioning
	Labelling
	Areas and rooms
	Room label
	Hatches
	Patterns
	Fillings
	Symbols
	Markers
	Fixed points
Plan layout	Frame
	Illustrations
	Scans
	Renderings

Table 2: Checklist for a computer visualization

Capacity	Hardware performance
	Software options
	Timeframe provided
Purpose of visualization	Design tool
	Intermediary presentation
	Final presentation
Level of detail in visualization	Close-up
	Building portrait
	Extended context (e.g. aerial shot)
Rendered scene	Choice of perspective, camera settings
	Image format
	Rendered object

	Lighting scenario
	Background or surroundings
Rendering parameters	if needed, rendering type (e.g. Raytrace, Phong, Gouraud, OpenGL, Z-Buffer etc.)
	Resolution
	Anti-aliasing
Surfaces	Colours
	Textures
	Reflexions
	Transparency

Table 3: Overview of CAD software

Program	Homepage
Allplan	www.nemetschek.com
ArchiCAD	www.graphisoft.com
ArCon	www.arcon-software.com
AutoCAD/Architectural Desktop/ Inventor/Revit Building	www.autodesk.com
BricsCad IntelliCAD	www.bricscad.com
CAD	www.malz-kassner.com
CATIA	www.catia.com
ideCAD	www.idecad.com
MicroStation	www.bentley.com
Reico CADDER	www.reico.de
RIB ARRIBA® CA3D	www.rib-software.com
SketchUp Pro	www.sketchup.com
Spirit	www.softtech.com
Solid Edge	www.ugs.com
TurboCAD	www.imsi.com

Table 4: Overview of rendering software

Programm	Homepage
3ds Max/VIZ	www.autodesk.com
Artlantis	www.graphisoft.com
Cinema 4D	www.maxon.net
Maya	www.alias.com
mental ray	www.mentalimages.com

PICTURE CREDITS

Figures 1, 4a, 12, 65, 88, 93:	Nemetschek AG, Munich – Allplan 2006
Figures 2, 3, 4b, 10, 11, 24, 69 , 71, 92:	Graphisoft – ArchiCAD 10
Figures 4c, 9, 25, 68, 94:	Autodesk GmbH Deutschland – Architectural Desktop 2007
Figures 53–55:	Bert Bielefeld, Isabella Skiba
Figures 73, 74, 76, 77, 78:	ch-quadrat architekten
Figure 75:	Frank Münstermann
Figure 81:	HKplus architekten
Figures 82–87:	HKplus architekten / the author
Figure 89:	Maxon Computer GmbH – Cinema 4D R10
All other figures:	The author

Series editor: Bert Bielefeld
Conception: Bert Bielefeld, Annette Gref
Layout and cover design: Muriel Comby
Translation from German into English:
Adam Blauhut, Joseph O'Donnell
English copy editing: Monica Buckland

Library of Congress Control Number: 2007923625

Bibliographic information published by
Die Deutsche Nationalbibliothek.
Die Deutsche Nationalbibliothek lists this
publication in the Deutsche Nationalbibliografie;
detailed bibliographic data are available on the
Internet at http://dnb.ddb.de.

This book is also available in a German
(ISBN 978-3-7643-8086-1) and a French
(ISBN 978-3-7643-8108-0) language edition.

© 2007 Birkhäuser Verlag AG
Basel · Boston · Berlin
P.O. Box 133, CH-4010 Basel, Switzerland
Part of Springer Science+Business Media

Printed on acid-free paper produced from
chlorine-free pulp. TCF ∞
Printed in Germany

ISBN 978-3-7643-8109-7
9 8 7 6 5 4 3 2 1   www.birkhauser.ch

ALSO AVAILABLE FROM BIRKHÄUSER: